COLLECTED AND NEW POEMS

Also by David Perman

History

Cublington, A Blueprint for Resistance (1973)
Change and the Churches: An Anatomy of Religion in Britain (1977)
A New History of Ware: its people and its buildings (2010)
The Malthouses of Ware (2017)
250 Years in Print: Stephen Austin & Sons of Hertford (2018)

Biography

Scott of Amwell: Dr Johnson's Quaker Critic (2001)
Stranger in a Borrowed Land: Lotte Moos and her writing (2012)
Islington Born and Bred: A Memoir of Childhood (2014)
A Square Peg in Bush House: Memories of a BBC Man (2021)

Poetry

The Buildings (1997)
A Wasp on the Stair (2004)
Scrap-Iron Words (2014)

David Perman

Collected and New Poems

Rockingham Press

Published in 2021 by
Rockingham Press
11 Musley Lane
Ware, Herts SG12 7EN

Copyright © David Perman, 2021

The right of David Perman to be identified as the author of this work has been asserted by him in accordance with Section 77 of the Copyright, Designs and Patents Act, 1988

British Library Catalogue-in-Print Data

A catalogue record for this book Is available from the British Library

ISBN 978-1-904851-837

I wish to dedicate this book
to many people, especially to
Danielle Hope,
my dearest friend and sharpest critic;

also to my inspiring three daughters,
Lucy, Sarah and Alice Perman;

to Patricia and the late William Oxley
for all their 'Poetry and Friendship'

and to my many friends and critics among
past and present members of
the Ware Poets.

ACKNOWLEDGEMENTS

Acknowledgements are due to the editors of
*Acumen, Ambit, The Frogmore Papers,
The Interpreter's House, Iota, The Listener,
london grip poetry, The London Magazine, Sofia*
and *Storm Brain Hippocrates anthology*
in which versions of some of these poems
were first published.

'Hospital' won the Eastern Arts Annual Report
Poetry Competition in 1994.

I would also like to thank my friends in the former
Tempest Poets for the critique of individual poems,
Frances Wilson and William Oxley
for their help and, finally, Danielle Hope
and Patricia Oxley for their support for this volume.

CONTENTS

The Buildings (1997)

Easter	13
Stubble Burning	14
Shooting Star	14
The King's Return	15
In Harness	16
Nude by the Fireplace	17
Sailing	18
A Rescued Man	19
A Place and No Place	20
Lateness	21
Stone-throwing, Ramallah	22
November 11th 1979	23
Last Innings	24
Grave Visiting	25
Harmonium	27
The Buildings	28

A Wasp on the Stair (2004)

Hospital	32
A Wasp on the Stair	33
Meeting the Ayatollah	34
How the Name is Pronounced	35
Double Take	36
The George the Fifth Look	37
Journey through a Changed Land	38
Social Climber	40
Barbarians	41
Appropriate	42
While Auden Lectured	43
The Tale of a Shirt	44
Titanic Tours	45
LOTTE POEMS	
Near the Edge	46
Icons	46
Confused	47

This is the Ice Floe	47
Immigrant	49
Teachers	50
Where did you go?	51
The Paradise Man	52
Sword-play	53
Blind Faith	54
The Apple Tree	55
Mydriasis	56
Her Hair among Other Things	57
Fourth World	58
Web	59
Red Squirrel	60
Friday Night	61
A Pregnant Bank	62
Under Warden Hill	63
World Without Elms	66
We receive but what we give	67
Elegy Written in the Hot Weather of July 1995	68
Abney Park Cemetery	69
London Nostalgia	70
Highbury Corner	71
The Grinling Neighbourhood	72
Real and Imagined – Cockington, South Devon	73
St. George's Ivychurch	74
Corked	75
Monemvasia, Peloponnese	76
A Day in Greece	77
Singapore	78
Raffles Hotel	79
GARDENS IN TOKYO	
1. Kiyosumi	80
2. Kitanomaru Park	81
3. Hama-rikyu	82
The Wasted Years by T.S. Hellavalot	83
The Man from Perth	84

Scrap-Iron Words (2014)

Distant Copse	85
Carless	86

The Patience of the Crocuses	87
Rivers Nursery, Sawbridgeworth	88
Thistles on Widbury	89
Blame	90
Dream Park	91
Normal	92
Intentionally Homeless	93
Maggie Merilyn	95
Meeting at Mortschach	96
Through Train	97
Hand in the Water	98
Queue	99
Proof	101
Grandeur and Greatness	102
Requiem	103
Rosie	104
Thrown Away	105
Morning	106
A Forgotten Meeting	107
There were Angels	109
Leipzig Monuments	110
Credo	112
Memory	113
Camphor	114
Buff	115
Me	116
Attitude	117
Berry Head Hotel	118
A Cautionary Tale	119
The Long Grass	120
Darwin and Mum	121
The Churchyard Yew	123
Lunching by the Sea of Galilee	124
Roadside Stop	125
Scrap-iron Words	126
Foldings	127
The Secret	128
In the Present	129
February	129
Down a Grassy Track	130
My Easter Rising	130

Uncollected Poems

Passing into Light	131
In the Garden of the Villa Cimbrone	132
Holiday Rain	133
Warnings of Severe Weather	133
Beastly Weather	134
The Fishmonger	135
Lazarus	136
George	137
Treasury	138
Into East Anglia	139
Wiping their Faces	140
The Rare Plant of Runnymede	141
John Wilburne Waiting	142
The Skylark	144
And Blackbirds shall inherit the Earth	144
A Not-so-Green Bird	145
Heron	146
Founders' Day	147
Five Fingers	148
Jackson's Wood	149
Post Wood	150
The Meads	151
Amwell Magna	153
Churston	154
The St. Pancras Way of Death	155
Kingsway	157
Winter Journey	158
Nancy's Funeral	159
Theo, 'loved by God'	160
This is the Record of John	161
Figures in a Landscape	163
Young Lions	164
Still an Issue	165
The Open Hand	165
A very old Love	166
Lady Wisdom	167
Heptonstall	168
Poems and Parsnips	169

Poppies	170
Hydrangea	170
Wanting Blue	171
Self-Portrait	172
A Close Shave	173
And there was Light	173
Life in the Gaps	174
Render	175
What's New?	176
Someone To Watch Over Me	177
The Tree within a Tree	179
Blossom Time	179
The Silk Cotton Tree	180
How it was	181
A Drastic Decline	182
B Movie	183
Because	184
Ghosts	185
Knife Crime	186

POEMS OF TRAVEL

The Samos Sea	188
Turkish Census Day	189
A GENOESE TRIPTYCH	
La Superba	190
Circonvalmonte	190
Pietra magica	191
RIVERS IN PORTUGAL	
1. The Douro	192
2. The Lima	192
3. The Minho	193
The Mendelssohn-Haus	194
In Search of JSB	194
Bach in the Kreuzkirche, Dresden	196
Nazareth	197
Jacob's Creek	197
Glebe Park, Camberra	198

STROKE POEMS 2018

Autonomy	199
Forgotten	200
Repartee	200

POEMS IN LOCKDOWN

Ash Wednesday 2020	202
Distancing	203
Disobediently Different	203
So much owed by so many	204
It had never gone away	205
Familiarly Unfamiliar	206
Back in Time	206
Be Prepared	207
Remembrance Day 2020	208

The Buildings (1997)

Easter

We talk across the oceans about the weather,
not knowing how to begin, when eyes cannot meet
or smiles over three thousand miles.
You speak of snow gusting over the lake.
Here a cold wind blows from the east
daffodils clam tight as if at night.

We touch each other with handfuls of news:
IRA threats, Apprentice Boys marching,
Israel's new war against Hezbollah.
It's Easter, all things should be new
not another wielding of wintry weapons.
We share a moment of despair.

The call is too costly for deeper thoughts.
There's much I want to say about what remains
really true for me and you,
how Ireland is more than guns and drums,
how bully boys' bellies grow fat
eyes too bleary to prime bombs,

how Israel's a land of promise not spite
and Hezbollah is not Allah,
how hope is not frozen under your snow
and peace must blossom
one day.   And then you say
the word we thought we'd never use.

Love may not be in the news
but it will open daffodils today.

Stubble-burning

It's been an airborne summer
as the binding waters fled
and earth rose up to catch the sun.
All life exists now in the browning,
parched fields, tanned skin,
even enamelled lady-birds
are dust-scuffed. But their bright
horde has been sucked away
with the moths and the long-legs.
Wasps have come and gone
and now the air is ruled by the sun
and the skeletal ash from stubble
burning. Before relief comes,
all life will dance in the fire.

Shooting Star

I wish I'd seen the shooting star they saw
from the island castle in that black sea
on that black night. It might have lifted
the headache, which wasn't ouzo but drilled
into brain crevices by the crazed floodlit chatter
of two drinkers, beating beams off each other, competing
to cast longer, sharper shadows as their talk ranged
over Third Sex (sans breast, sans balls, sans everything),
to mad mothers, suicides, stolen children,
and the drugs they knew as well as faces
of chat-show hostesses. Two drinkers
flirting with madness and with each other,
the damaged child thrusting out as a woman,
the damaged woman curling back as a child.
Two lamps of unequal size but similar intensity,
burning themselves out in the dark night
on an island in a black sea. The shooting
star came and died in the blink of an eye.
I did not see it, the headache remained.

The King's Return

Home-come to a place of holy ground,
wholly his at least, making his heart pound
with draughts of his native air.
Yes, by Jove, this is it!   He's here,
the King returned.   Holding his ground.

No longer making for Ashdod,
sighting the enemy through a salted iron port
while war legs braced the slimy planks.
(What matter if the port was double Perspex,
condensation-dribbled, and the planks
steel-ribbed and carpet ash-trod?)

Here, children!   Run, jump up and kiss him,
you creatures of his flesh and bone!
Come wife, into the circle come,
let him hear how much you missed him.
Make a fuss of your king come home!

Everyone knows in triumph he's come
for messengers, troubadours must have sung
his fabled exploits in the royal siege.
(Oh, what matter if merely the office rang
to say his flight was delayed in Liege?)
He's home.   That's the thing,
a travelling, globe-stepping man is home.

So approach and all the booty see
that he's brought back from cloudless climes.
(What if the scent was duty-free
and these souvenirs seen a dozen times?)
Do you expect him to exchange glories
for the cosy reading of bedtime stories
and the warlike mass of the Thracian ships
for command of a trolley on shopping trips?

So he came to his own, who kissed him not.
His triumph they denied, instead they applied

a cold wet poultice to his risen pride.
The bills unpaid, ailments still uncured
and repairs overdue to stem the rot
were the greeting they gave their returning lord.
So, pressed by new foes on every side

the king laid about him with his sword.
What matter if he used just the cutting word?

In Harness

What causes such pain between the traces?
Is it that two remain close-harnessed
when most the fraying thongs have snapped
and high-kicked apart.
Or was the matching wrong from the start?

I've heard say by some who claim to know
that like with like run best
between the shafts and it can only be
asking for trouble
a handsome, fine-nosed breed to couple
with a workhorse, however big its heart.

The self-same experts express surprise
that these two came so far together.
But it's not the partner that wounds the side:
it's the constant strain
and the tight-drawn leather.

Nude by the Fireplace

Each morning I watch you re-enact
that Bonnard painting before my eyes.
You snatch at the curtains for a slice
of morning, then turn your back
upon me as you dress. But such
modesty is futile, for the glow
on those dorsal hills, smooth and low,
energises my longing as much

as the contrasts of shade and fire
in the peaks and valleys you conceal.
In a quick gesture, you reveal
the landscape of my desire
which I long to reach and hold,
but the impressioned picture vanishes;
your swift dressing tarnishes
with dull cloth your body's gold.

You depart and leave me realising
that through the dark hours we lay
a stretched finger's touch away
while desire lay unrecognising.
We slept as prisoners of yesterday
and were free, only when we woke;
but already I have seen you take
the bond-clothes of another day.

Sailing

I'm a clean sailor now:
nothing has been thrown overboard for months.
In fact nothing has been consumed

to create new flotsam.
Yet there it stays.   The accusing wake
stretching, narrowing to the horizon,

never left behind.   I had
long relationships with those trash clusters
all surrounded by guilty slicks --

or is that a trick of the light?
Those bobbing alone were brief encounters,
some plastic bright and buoyant,

most simply rubbish
all keeping pace as I watch.
I see them every day and can tell

the colour and content
of them all -- even the most distant.
I doubt if I will take on fresh supplies,

flotsam is all I have.
Maybe that's why it never leaves me.
I'd take it on board again if I could.

A Rescued Man

The child's eyes widen as chips
are put before it; an old man
nods, grins, pretends to eat one –
I want to hug them both, buy teas
for the whole caff, do a run
and a hundred handstands, touch trees –
as only a rescued man can.

I can't say what lies behind my
elation – ropes and cupboard walls,
or timbers crashing in the blazing block,
the ocean crushing wreck against rock
or a snow-hole high in the frozen span –
I drink my amnesia by the mug-full,
as only a rescued man can.

I cannot buttonhole any strangers
with what I've been through, or recommend
my saviours for a popular medal –
the fireman, psychiatrist or priest,
paramedic or rubbered lifeboatman –
I just live and savour this present feeling
as only a rescued man can.

I've lived most of my life as a hero,
a leader, genius, an upcoming man,
I've been feared and acknowledged,
admired, flattered and savaged
as a cut above the ordinary man –
now I sit unnoticed, noticing,
as only a rescued man can.

A Place and No Place

Since my pagan eyes were pledged
to the blind worship of your face,
I had not seen that special place,
with wild chervil and charlock edged
where the road dips to a layby
then climbs to the church's verdigris wedge.

From that spire, the valley falls below
through tussocked meadows and reaches
a stream, hidden by blood-stained beeches
and hawthorn, blossom-clumped like snow.
Then up again to that lozenge field
of ripening rape, unbelievably yellow.

As that sharp diamond sliced
my sight, the shining icon of your face
was veiled. You had no place
there, nor could that valley apprise
the tumbling rivers of your mind
or flashing cascade of your eyes.

For the power of that gentle place
was greater than the human ties
I'd vowed to sever in your eyes
and while I know that true faith
requires no seeing, I have to find
that valley somewhere in your face.

Lateness

Scientists in California have discovered
the gene that causes lateness
-- in fact it was discovered
five years ago.

In Britain alone lateness //
costs industry £12 billion
and results in
10,000 cold dinners,
6,327 divorces,
11,322 chewed fingernails -- at least --
and 71 cancelled funerals.

The Secretary of State has announced
a national lateness screening programme
amid opposition cries of
too much and too soon,
while the right-wing
not-nature-but-nurture group
is demanding custodial sentences
for three-time latecomers.

An editorial in *Marxism Today* pronounced
punctuality the politeness of kings --
thus undemocratic.
The *British Psychological Journal*
said punctual people were pessimists.
The *Church Times* said theologians
believed lateness to be divine,
pointing out that man was not
created until the seventh day.
They were meeting of course ...
in Byzantium.

Stone-throwing, Ramallah

He runs, leaps, feet tread
air, the arm's slung back,
eyes take aim. He could be
a javelin-thrower on a frieze
but for the trainers and jeans.

They say it's now ritual
this young men's artillery against
riot shields and armoured cars –
from the roadside pieces of
concrete, breeze-block, best of all

the local rock. The action's ancient
only the technique has changed:
to stone a Stephen or Magdalene
the rock was held shoulder-high
and hurled down by a tight circle.

A few rocks, perhaps two per thousand,
have survived chariot wheels,
crusaders' hooves and tanks to be
always available by the road –
ancient ritual, hallowed stones.

November 11th 1979

(60 years after the first Remembrance Day)

The silence is slipped between the hit tunes
like old cheese in a crispbread sandwich
with the scraping of a tangey bugle
to make it more palatable.
But it's not silence of course –
there's "atmosphere", a discreet cough
from an engineer to show the equipment's functioning
and what's a two-minute silence
when you hear it revving along on the car stereo?
At one time, everything stopped.
Men stood by the car doors, trilbies doffed,
Grandad erect near the wireless, children's heads bowed
waiting for the boom of the guns from Land's End
to John O'Groats.
Anyone who moved was a traitor.
But that was before Wonderful Radio One
before disc jockeys and Caroline
before the Beatles, the Stones, Bob Dylan and
Jimmy Hendrix.
Even before Bill Haley. But we still do it,
the two-minute memory not for the
Kampuchean dead or Afghanistan or the Ogaden
not even for Belfast, Aden, Arnhem and the Imjin.
It's only for the kids of Flanders
senseless to the strong beat of the Big Bertha Band
whose youth culture fertilised the poppies
in the unsilent mud.

Last Innings

i.m. John Fletcher, Town Clerk

He's such a private man, we say,
shy at the visitors gathering by his bed;
shocked by the image we bring away.

With books on cricket he passes the day,
the only known commitment he ever had;
he's such a private man, we say.

He doesn't complain at all at the way
his neck has swelled to a cricket ball red;
shocked by the image we bring away.

If only he had let some woman lay
hands on the smoke-stained life he lived;
he's such a private man we say.

He's losing weight each passing day
though with piped vitamins he's being fed;
shocked by the image we bring away.

He's such a very private man, we say,
shy at the visitors gathering by his bed;
we know he may not last another day,
shocked by the image we bring away.

Grave Visiting

I've come to show Mum my new car.
If she raises her chin above
the crocuses, last year's burnt out
saxifrage, the uncut lawns
she'll just see it between the headstones.

I like to tell her of my success.
If she could speak, she'd say "lovely dear"
with a faint frown. She never did like
cars and would grip the headrest or
my shoulder, saying "you're going too fast".

One similar February day she stood
and watched a car speed past
then stepped in front of another.
She never did like cars -- though Dad did
and would have loved one, but for

his eyes and the expense. I can't
show it to him, he's fourteen years
below. But she'll tell him about it.
She always told him everything.
Even afterwards.

*

I don't believe they're still here,
sorted C of E one side, the rest the other
in the council's well-kept Woodwell cemetery.
I used to bring her here for her
Sunday fussing over Dad's grave.

She'd dart forward, bend and dig,
stretch, dig and hoe, legs akimbo.
I imagined Dad grinning
as he looked up her skirt
-- a Stanley Spencer Resurrection.

I still smile at her ways,

like her pained Gospel Hall reaction
on that segregated side of the park
at the row of Catholic graves behind,
the dinky virgin in the plastic bubble,

the wheelbarrow carrying a slab: *we have
prayed for you at the holy grotto,*
the four young tinkers playing
shirt-sleeved cards on a parent's grave.
I too say *how terrible,* sweetening the loss.

*

I fuss at tidying the grave as she
used to, stuff stiff green stems into bent
aluminium, then stand back and read.
The names, dates are strong and clear
but my new flowers hide the last
words, the first French I ever knew,
the secret I share with them: *Je t'aime,*
written in his proud copperplate
on a forces' aerogram from Bombay,
stiff, small and grey with a faint
Taj Majal in the top right-hand corner.

Je t'aime.   Je t'aime.

Harmonium

On a bright June evening with no need of lights
we laboured a pram chassis bearing a load
which wobbled and creaked and hissed out odd notes,
a small whistling man and a tall boy in shorts
pushing a harmonium up Balls Pond Road.

It came from the Gospel Hall where the fat woman
who played it at meetings insisted the need
for something electric which could hold its own
against Hallelujahs and shouts of Amen
in place of the harmonium in Balls Pond Road.

We went over tram lines and felt the load lurch
we passed curious people who stared and smiled
and the grunts of an organ came out of a church
to greet its small cousin up on its perch,
the harmonium pushed up Balls Pond Road.

I knew that once home with patches he'd start
repairing the bellows while playing a chord,
just as he'd patched up the old wooden flute
with a four-inch split that had once made it mute,
so the harmonium in Balls Pond Road.

He was no collector, just anxious to play –
I found an old letter after he died
from a piccolo salesman regretting to say
that prison would follow his failure to pay –
the free harmonium in Balls Pond Road.

I outgrew his music, bought records instead
and made enough money so that I could afford
to buy any instrument he ever desired.
But nothing can bring back the concert we shared
pushing a harmonium up Balls Pond Road.

THE BUILDINGS

Samuel Lewis

In a book on Islington I saw my aunt's back window,
not as she knew it but back-clothing Laycock's Dairy,
a rural square resisting terraces for clerks to give
Victorian villas milk for their morning tea.
But the dairy could not baulk the barracks of the poor,
built alliteratively over its fields -- Liverpool Buildings first,
then Lewis Buildings, Laycock Mansions last,
three escarpments to my child's eye squeezing
the twisting street into a canyon of shadows.

Samuel Lewis built highest and best
in his Trust Dwellings for the Poor
with curving cornices, deck upon deck of proud
windows, six great galleons ready to sail
up Liverpool Road to the New World,
and everywhere warm brick and fiery tiles,
which glowed warmer than any grate,
tiles treasured, touched by sticky fingers but
wiped always at least once a week,
tiles framing the detached drying-room
with hot pipes under the creaking catwalk
where week by week our mothers
hung the bag-wash carefully away
from the sheets of others,
tiles coralling everything in undulating
orange walls as if the philanthropist had
underlined his work in sepia ink.

Shelters

Near the drying room was Hitler's bunker
who was never there when needed
but always hunting small boys who
climbed the plane trees in what we
called gardens or built makeshift
shelters among the sooty privets.

The street canyon is now one-sided –
Lewis Buildings reigns alone
opposite so-called social or
sheltered housing.   Sure we were
social and they did give us shelters
built in the Battle of Britain but
overshadowed by the buildings
so that no one used them except
for a quick pee or hunting rats.
In one shelter Joe Gilbert said a girl
was showing what she had up her skirt
but I was afraid of the dark.
Then the shelters were demolished
leaving cement squares which served us
as football fields and cricket pitches.
They had pensioned off Hitler
and erected no ball games signs
but balls still bounced in the buildings.

Curtain

It hung there to hide the passage
and the brown-stained bedroom doors,
shiny, the colour of sterilised milk.
It sagged from its plastic coated wire
even before our daily tugs
to let more light in at night.

I lived in the bedroom for fourteen years
but for centuries behind the curtain,
swishing it aside to take a boyish bow,
with bedspread cape, twisted poker sword,
stabbing a Polonius through its arras,
finding a crack to peep at aunts chatting
on leather chairs and other women
too fat to enter my harem drapes.

Mornings were arms full of books,
moving the folds with my nose
and sneezing the dust of dreams

down the stone stairs outside.
Evenings were expectation as
I unveiled Florentine fresco,
a secret door, answer to exams,
a damsel dressed in damask.

Then a friend died and his coffin passed
through a curtain to emerge
as a plastic casket in his sister's arms.
The next day I lit a match
and my curtain melted
to the floor at my feet.

Modernisation

Over the balcony it came, cascading glass
making matchwood of the partitions,
the room that served us as kitchen,
bathroom, study, refuge,
collapsed into a skip.
It was always in danger of imploding.
Every morning we all pushed back
those walls, Dad shaving while
Mum laid breakfast on the table
pushed hard against the boiler
while we queued to use the loo
out on the balcony by the coal.
Inside that green wood
I studied for A levels, letting the
Third Programme hold the walls apart,
Glyn Houston conjuring up Llareggub,
Gielgud making that cell his court,
Deller and Jennifer Vyvyan
magicking a forest with music.

But on bath nights the walls
felt bold enough to move
and conspired with the bath top,
thick as a church door, as it was
hauled up and clamped to the wall,
its stumps hanging like the legs

of a slaughtered sow over my white body.
Only alertness and will power
prevented it falling to encase me
in the coffin that the room wanted,
its green paint ready to cover
my early grave like grass.

I didn't see the bath come out.
It must have been sold to a scrapyard.
The walls imagine they've now won,
as they clasp each other
in the embrace they sought for years,
window against window,
wood against wood.
There's not an inch of life between them.

Going Back

Returning is always a risk, that the old
print will be obliterated by the brochure
colours of today, of the real world
where mistakes have been undone economically,
where old values may be proved false.
Outside changes are dramatic, chastening:
the austere council flats flattened,
replaced by designer mounds of grass,
the rushing street dammed to a backwater.
The buildings remain, with railings re-erected --
six proud women anchored in black lace-ups;
there are padlocks on the drying room,
entry buttons outshine the burnished tiles,
and new rolled asphalt's everywhere --
poverty preserved in asphalt.   But is it?
We knew we were poor because it said so
in carved stone.   It was no more than a label
because we had our dreams and though men in
sharp suits could pay key money for a pad
they did not tread on our dreams.

A Wasp on the Stair (2004)

Hospital

Temple of Health – hallowed by action,
the knife, the steady hand and magic
laser beam. Words are a form of unction,
a colour rubric on the electronics:
I'll just take your blood pressure – beep, beep.
A theatre where words have walk-on parts:
A tiny prick, then you'll be asleep.

So close it down, says the government,
mothball the cash-devouring wards.
With keyhole cuts, consumers will want
to be treated in High Street surgery shops,
all in a day, or even an hour –
ignoring what every patient knows
that words too have a healing power.

In this general surgical ward, all is
not silent suffering. The mobile push
their stories before them like shopping trolleys;
and in drip-fed beds, eyes are searching
for words. Jimmy, with bowel cancer –
a Scottish cook who'll cook no more –
has a hundred questions requiring answer.

Les shouts loudly: *where's that bell?*
He came for an op and had a stroke.
*What bell, love? I can't hear a bell.
I need the bell – oh, deary, deary me!
There's no – oh, you mean a bowl!*
So vocabulary becomes a branch of health
when words have power to make him whole.

A Wasp on the Stair

For Albie Sachs

A wasp on the stair, a yellow
ball greying in the dust – dead I know
but picked up carefully by a wing
in case the sting lives on.
On the radio life under apartheid
by an Afrikaans liberal lawyer
who holds the record for the longest
time in solitary. It broke him he says
but a car bomb blew optimism back
into his life – at the cost of a limb
and an eye.

Apartheid is dead, we know.
He tells of meeting his interrogator and
shaking his hand but could not do
the same for the man who primed
the bomb. It's now November
and solitary wasps have been
appearing in the bedrooms, mostly
dead, picked up carefully
by a wing – in case the sting lives on.
I must find where the nest is
before the spring.

Meeting the Ayatollah

*In 1979, the writer went with a BBC Iranian colleague,
Ferri Jahed, to interview opponents of the Shah of Iran.*

A cold coming we had of it.
We left the steamy corridors of Paris
crowded with clansmen and children,
where speeches were tremendous, bodyguards nervous,
and come out on an evening autoroute
to a village and a villa.   The CRS
stopped every vehicle, verifying passes;
a woman with a sunset of red hair
peered over a wall while her hound
pee-ed against it – patriotically.

   Within, students stamping their feet,
mullahs stared – all men, of course – and
murmured approval of our mission and microphones,
gave us strong tea, showed us how to suck it
through crude sugar lumps.
We offered cigarettes; but the Imam's son-in-law
smoked his own – mentholated, duty-free.
And then we entered, an Englishman
and three Iranians, Ferri,
Ashraggi, the son-in-law, and Yazdi,
devout Muslim from the name of a Magus.

   All this was a long time ago, but I remember
others sitting, crowding behind, eager
as if at a boxing match; Ferri
and I squatted, studying typed out questions,
testing the mike: *one, two, three, four.*
Khomeini entered and squatted close,
touchably close, a mere brush and ....
but my hand would have withered!
I pressed the button and spoke and Ferri
translated. The bearded face before us
barely looked up, studying a pencilled exercise

book before it spoke. One answer followed
another, rising in intensity – I know no Farsi
but did hear the words America, Reza Shah,
sensed from the tightness in Ferri's fists
that this was a curse akin
to destruction by sword, famine and pestilence.
We were sitting before Jeremiah.
It would have been better had we never been born.

    We got it all on tape, went home
and played it back endlessly – to experts,
incredulous colleagues, bosses. Then we broadcast it --
not my words, I merely framed the questions
which the Ayatollah Khomeini ignored and
the rest is already history. You're surprised
that I feel at ease with it all.
Were we makers of history, or just pawns,
one small step in the march of time?
Who now remembers the other carpenter
who specialised in crosses or the pale youth
who bought matches for the Emperor Nero?

How the Name is Pronounced

Gin-and-tonic at the bar
to radio reporter from afar:
"You've met this ayatollah feller –
how d'you pronounce the name of the chap?
Is it Khó-many like a dry homily
or Kho-máiny – as with a maniac?
Get my meaning?" said he with a slap.
"Neither. The stress is equal throughout:
Khó-méi-ní." "But that sounds
like a revolutionary shout."
"Well, that's how the name is pronounced."

Double Take

Yes, it was frightening but exciting too.
We ran across fifty metres of open ground
– *oh at least a hundred* – right in front
of their guns. It was a miracle they didn't
open fire. My hair stood on end.
I had goose pimples all over.

The papers we carried cost us a week's
rations – *a year's wages* – and the clothes
were too big, too baggy. *Certainly too big.*
They smelled foreign but everything that
went on was foreign.

We hid in straw – *under piles of vegetables.*
At the border soldiers poked with their sticks –
not sticks, they were bayonets – poking deep,
                              this way and that.
One of them tore my sleeve. Here's the tear, the scratch.

Then we were shut up for eighteen hours –
more like 24 – in that metal container
without bread or water. *Precious little air.*
Forbidden to talk or move in case
they heard us. *It was creepy – in case*
the guards heard us.

When we reached these shores, people couldn't
believe we had done it. I went to the Palace
                              and was decorated.
When we reached these shores, I was detained and
sent to a camp in the north country.

I was a hero, I had escaped from an evil enemy.
Now I am a magistrate. I uphold the rule of law.
I was an asylum seeker, escaping persecution.
I had faith in this country's rule of law.

You are <u>at best</u> an economic migrant, at worst

unhealthy, immoral, perhaps criminal
even a terrorist —
we must send you back.

I am an asylum seeker, fleeing an evil enemy.

No. <u>We</u> were the ones who fled the evil enemy.
<u>You</u> are a sponger.

<u>You</u> *are an oppressor.*

We have nothing in common.
We will send you back.

The George the Fifth Look

Unmoved he reads his paper
while mothers struggle with buggies
and howling youngsters strap-swing
about his ears – pink, private ears
lurking behind the grey silk curtain
which joins to a Saxe-Coburg tache
and a stylish Windsor beard.
It's the George the Fifth look.
The fringed eyes would be so kind
if they ever once looked up
at children, at general strikers or
an eldest son adulterating,
in preparation for abdicating.
He turns now to the stamp-collectors' page
and does an eyelash smile.
Mm.   Not a bad likeness.

Journey through a Changed Land

After 9-11

The pandas were real cute, climbing an' wrestling
barely a broom handle's length away,
as my mamma used to say:
the kids, my son's – Jake's son's –
kids squealed with delight:
they'll be going back tonight
for 'Boo in the Zoo' – the ghosts and bone men
all lit up, the wolves howling and owls a-hooting:
that'll sure make 'em squeal. They talked
of cancelling Hallowe'en, 'cause of what happened
– the other thing that happened – in September.
The pumpkin growers wouldna let 'em, said son John;
they're just party poopers, said little Sam, and
we laughed – the first time I'd laughed since
September the Eighth. Yeah Jake passed away
three days before you know what: I'm kinda glad
he didna see it though I woulda liked him aside me
on the couch to explain it all.

Hey but I almost missed the turn-off and
went to Trenton, where nobody wants a go now
'cause of the anthrax – that comes a following that
Buick with the nodding Shepherd in the winda
daydreaming of pandas. We used to have a Buick.

They showed this ceremony where Richard Gere
spoke of forgiving and they booed him:
Jake woulda done too, never liked *American Gigolo*,
never liked Buddhists – we don't have many in Kentucky.
Can you forgive without forgetting, would I forgive
if Jake had been in the Trade Centre instead of a bed,
do I forgive the surgeons, the tobacco giants, or him?
He had a fag in his mouth when I met him,
said he only took it out to drink and sleep
then took it out and kissed me. Jake!
They say everything changed on September 11

but it never changed back for me.
It's kinda strange, as if the whole world has joined
my grief though course I would rather they hadn't,
it's also lonely being in a deep grievin' world
for the wrong reason, though people are kindly
'cause of what happened, like. Like I rang
the Yankee Stadium and thought they'd refuse
tell me to go take a jump in the Hudson
but they musta assumed I was a Ground Zero
widow. "Just bring us the casket, ma'am,
you're not the first, we'll do everything necessary."

The colours of Fall are so wonderful
in New Jersey, so much brighter than Kentucky.
Jake woulda loved to see them. I won't take
the Lincoln Tunnel: he wouldna want
to see that skyline ... now.

Social Climber

He earned his tag on the nursery wall
daubed his way in and out of school
to the District Line and single-handed
all its silver carriages branded
with bright mauve monograms on each door
then after a single brush with the law
set a new record for a boy of nine –
twenty-eight bridges on the A39.

Recruited to a government rehab scheme
as leader of his graffiti team
he was given a blank wall – courtesy
of Bright-Colour-Single-Coat plc –
on which to make a tentative start
in educating himself in art,
introduced to women and wine
took a late degree in graphic design

– a <u>too</u> late degree for that rehearsal
in fine art was not commercial:
now every member of his college set
was designing sites for the internet
and so he retreated to SW9
hoping to sign the whole District Line
only to find that since his day
trains had been treated with anti-paint spray.

Eventually our hero found his niche
working high on a cathedral perch
restoring corbels and ancient gargoyles
in tempera, gouache and in oils
with old grotesquenesses which come
from the start of the last millennium
a practice, of course, never shunned
by the English Heritage Lottery Fund.

Barbarians

Today's lecture concerns artefacts
from Second Millennium Britain –
we begin with a tall black box.
You may think it resembles a coffin
the latest research shows it was –
a conveyance to crematoria
as automotive hearses failed
through congestion on the roads.

Note the inscription *Wheel – i.e.b – in*
the subject of much learned discussion.
Shanghai Professor Wang Liu
thought an "ieb" was a water-fowl:
we'll be returning later to Liu.
We can now state it was not *i.e.b.*
but *one-e.b.* for *one expired body* –
a mixture of numerals and initials
found on pre-2000 websites.
It was for wheeling the body in
– note the lugs for tipping it out.
Britons showed no respect for their ancestors.

Professor Liu thought *i.e.b.* was a fowl
from his research into our second object
this cage on wheels, <u>always</u> found
in rivers and canals. We know
from avian skeletons nearby
it was there for coots to nest in.
Bird-loving Britons gave names
to these cages – the "safeway" and
the "as-da" (their slang for "has to").
Why the wheels? They were to stop
rats from gaining a foothold.

Our third object shows a condition
experienced increasingly at the
Millennium – drought. This funnel
collected rainwater along roads.

It was coloured red as a warning
that the water had to be boiled
because of atmospheric pollution.

All three objects show the reliance
of the Millenarians on materials
which did not degrade. They did
do some recycling and indeed
their books have not survived
save as electronic images.
But these important artefacts
were strictly non-biodegradable.
That is fortunate for us or we
would not understand the ways
of these curious distant cousins
of our North American slaves.

Appropriate

i.m. Ken Smith, poet

Appropriate it was a shed where he launched
his last time ship, that upside-down dory
or dhow to transport home his treasures –
not the tripe and trinkets of so-called history
but histories of fellow creatures
who'd given him that look of recognition
he'd met in lounges, trains and taxis,
remembered rooms, creatures he'd rescued –
but who rescued whom? – to be shipped
or stowed away for asylum in the all-faith
all-purpose all singing and dancing temple
he'd built at East of the Wall Ham
where mice and spiders served as acolytes
where masks marked the via dolorosa
and a High Priestess gave love and roll-ups.

While Auden lectured

"The young poet ... makes little distinction between a book, a country walk and a kiss. All are equally experiences to store away in his memory."
                               W.H. Auden *

Only the kiss clings to my fingertips
as I trawl through memories
of those autumn months – the lips
of a bosomy nurse easy to talk to,
met at a Free Church freshers' hop
unfrequented by college girls,
locked up by eleven o'clock.

The Thirties rebel in gown and hood
said poems were acts of worship
then sat mornings a sad-eyed Buddha
awaiting acneed poets' coffees
in the Cadena.   I longed to converse
but the shaman sat in the shadow
cast by my radiant nurse.

But it was no time for poetising
with Eden in Suez, Russians in Buda
and Dennis Potter's anger rising
at the condescension of cloistered dons;
so we drank and talked and drank instead,
my nurse left Oxford and I went on
studying poets who were dead.

*   His inaugural lecture as Oxford Professor of Poetry in
     The Dyer's Hand and other essays (1963), p. 43.

The Tale of a Shirt

There's a shirt I have a problem with:
or ... it has a problem with me.
I bought it in Naples, Florida,
where New Yorkers go to die
from a girl in the Serendipity Shop
for two dollars and a smile.

It's Sea Island cotton with a faint stripe,
and a label from Hathaway's
followed by a letter and number code,
(the serial number of the shirt)
and a distinctive executive's laundry mark
picked out in blood-red thread.

The shirt is at its happiest when
it's ironed and buttoned and hung.
Then I see it beginning to preen itself
for leveraged Wall Street deals
that swell the assets of millionaires
with the closure of factories and mills.

It yearns to cover Herculean limbs
in its fine poisonous folds.
My thin white neck makes it squirm
and shrink back out of sight
beneath my sweater with the hole in the arm.
– I dare not wear it with a suit.

Titanic Tours

We dread the sea but trust
its discretion. If not fire or wood
to clasp our loved ones in earth,
we grant them watery graves
resting at depths never yet dug,
guarded by creatures blind as night.

We did not count on floodlights,
cable-hung cameras or greedy
gantries grabbing at plates
pierced by portholes to amuse
tourists tired of roulette,
or suits high up in New York
touting Titanic souvenirs.

Another day in another sea
divers videoed the Derbyshire
not to exploit, only to see
why she suddenly snapped in two.
The families needed to know
why men died, who was to blame --
but as they viewed each saw
the dead walk to and fro.

So Titanic tourists as you've paid
for an experience quite unique,
when you lie in your cabin bed
may nightmares rock your sleep
may lights all fade, cables break,
no portholes pierce the waves,
just one priceless souvenir
the dead dancing as you wake.

LOTTE POEMS

Near the Edge

She sat on the bed overlooking the tracks,
told him she'd tried to kill herself.
Old women came close -- peering like ships'
lights trying to penetrate a coastal fog.

"But I wasn't very efficient!" She squeezed
a smile of self-knowledge: the pills were old
with instructions written in Portuguese,
bought across the counter on holiday.

The fog lifted. She complained of screams,
in the night, thieving, the indignity of students
crowding her in consultation rooms.
She said she was legally free to go.

But confusion was now enveloping him.
Had she intended death or just a cry
for help and revenge on all of them,
friends, children, the needless young?

He wanted to see her as a child,
testing the wind-swept edge, more daring than
leaping -- otherwise he knew he must hold
her tight and never dare let go again.

Icons

She worshipped her parents' icons, resolved
to live by them but even as a child was aware
they could not protect her – not Rosa,
eloquent, limping, diminutive mega-star
of the workers, martyred by soldiers, dumped

in the Landwehr Canal – not Goethe whose bust

had pride of place in the parlour until bumped
by a fidgety child and converted to dust.
Her father comforted her, affirmed the culture
of their Fatherland was much greater than
                                        any piece of stone.
These were their icons, heroes for the post-war era,
their role models, <u>not</u> their religion: they had none –
until soldiers pinned yellow stars to their coats.
By then their daughters were in foreign parts.

Confused

She must not go home, said the nurse,
she's confused, she'll fall or worse.
Her carer had been called away,
the locum lost the key, called to Lotte
to open the door. But she didn't
get out of bed – incontinence
at ninety-three even is embarrassing.
So the police were called of course
and an entry made by force.
In hospital when she refused treatment,
they sedated her. She became confused.

Weeks later the television
coughs up cartoons and she asks:
What is this place?
It is not a prison, is it? *No.*
It is not a hospital? *No.*
It is not a hotel? *No.*
Then what is it?
It's an assessment centre.
I don't want to be assessed,
I want to go home.

This is the Ice Floe

We had been discussing politics –
slowly for it takes her time to tune her mind

to the world outside –
when Connie the carer came.
How's my little Lottie today?
and the little white head was engulfed
in breasts and arms for Connie is as big
and Irish as the nurses are black.

Fingers fiddled with the hearing aid
– *you need another battery* – pulled at hair
that needed cutting, again clasped
her charge to her chest. Over and above it all
Connie confided her diagnosis
in dramatic lip movements whose sound
was drowned by the television.

Lotte smiled like a cherubic child
and I remembered her poem,
'Old People's Home':

Now the bird has been caught
Now the net's been drawn tight
Four narrow walls
And nowhere to hide.

This is the ice floe
That will float you to death
Learn to say 'Thank you'
Under your breath.

Immigrant

I shun them, those born
in my country. I hate their talk of
polite policemen with buttoned-up
collars, slow-moving cars with
bucket-seats or running boards,
wireless nights with
Henry Hall, *The Navy Lark*.

I won't go with them
idle window-shopping
immigrants of the past.
My ear is pierced
I wear leather, tight jeans,
and spurn flannels hanging
from paunch-stretched braces.
I'll not dead-head the garden,
go out for a Sunday drive,
snooze before game-shows,
eat sliced-bread cut cornerwise,
dream of trams and steam-trains,
and then search for a lost collar stud
in a cold bedroom.

But when someone asks
who was Attlee,
where was Aden,
when Finzi is forgotten,
Browning never read,
and no one's worth their word,
when graffiti grows like grass,
cars grind bumper to bumper
and the only food is a kebab,
I recall the crossing of that
wide ocean of war and
wonder how it would have been
if we could have stayed --
only then do I recall the pollution
of class we breathed in every day.

Teachers

My memory is they were tired,
tired pre-war men – and bald.
Tired of wading through an adolescent tide
in clapped-out classrooms – built
for Victorian missionaries' daughters
to force-feed French, Latin verbs,
tables and how to construe a sentence.

Tired of London smog, the slummy
sliding of cockney vowels, chalky fingers
on faded gowns, gouged desks,
broken books, inkwells flooding
and chewing gum everywhere.
Tired of herding the cringing
crowd up the hills of the School Cert.

And they were bald to a man –
even Mrs. Gould, soft and freckled
under her blouses, as she beat time,
sang out scales and sonata form,
even she aspired to baldness.

They were tired, but they were proud.
Proud to be known as sir and ma'am.
proud of knowledge, achievement,
to be masters in a meritocratic world.
And we learned more from their pride
than the books which – like them – were tired.

Where did you go?

i.m. Edward Goodrham Taylor, priest

Hard to visualise you in Hackney
now suburbed with Dacca and Istanbul:
what would they make of a priest
in a leather-lined long-nosed Morris?

Impossible now the school has gone
to see you in the study by the kitchens
expounding Schweitzer on the human Jesus
beating the air with thick haired fingers
to vinyl Vaughan Williams songs.

You vanished while my back was turned
while my front faced manhood's
jealous joys and distractions.

But somewhere west of Honiton
there's a field scored with bell-tent rings
where a bearlike man in baggy shorts
calls boys to a marquee
and they come with faces aflame –
worrying then and now to the worldly wise
who never knew your love.

The Paradise Man

i.m. William Oxley, poet

He leads us out of town by the steepest
hill forging ahead like Moses
his stick numbering the steps
to the promised land.   Our hearts beat.

There is grandeur in this knot of coast
from Brixham to the indented Dart –
downland sweeping up and over
Sharkham Point balanced above
bouldered coves the spreading sea.
Then the thrust of hills – he says:
"Fifteen minutes of agony and it's over"
but the deep-creased coastal path
continues – Mansands to Scabbacombe
Pudcombe to Mill Bay Cove.   Paradise
hard won for dismayed lives
lived mainly on the level.

Glimpses of Paradise is his manuscript title:
I long to know if these aching Devon views
constitute a quest fulfilled
Nature's late balm on wounds
he felt when ripped from a childhood
beside northern woods and streams.
Words climb to that conclusion
and then retreat – and his poems repeat
the thought (and doubt) that Nature
gives a broad hint of what's beyond
but is not Paradise's last repose.

So on he goes, now clambering
up a steep incline while we drop back
admiring vetch, a purple emperor.
Why does he climb so fast?   What fear
is in his mind?   Could the next summit
be the dismaying last as a sea fog

settles on the sunlit shore?   Could he
have been mistaken in memory's joy?
Worst of all, could philistines have flooded
the valley with that accountant's dream
a caravan park?   It is only by this urgent audit
that the Paradise Man will know.

Sword-play

No glint no gleam, there is
no flash of steel in such surroundings –
the New Year sun, a log fire, memories
of a long lunch – as the blade's length
slides from its sheath and makes its presence
felt between two friends,
the physician collector of kukris and kris-es
and the academic author who declines to take
or touch the sword proffered by his friend.

They respect each other in every respect
but this; they recall a dinner years before
– in summer, beside the sea – when one
invited the other to see his samurai
swords and sashes and armour and was
rebuffed in reply. Was it principle or family
memories that made the author
so passionate in condemning such swords
as the wartime weapons of barbarous
bushido? Or was it the strong Ligurian wine?
For years they corresponded
about the morality of such things, fencing
with words on paper and phone ... until now.

The author watches, praying that
the tale that a drawn blade must draw blood
is not true. His friend caresses the curved
steel with a silken skein, replaces it
in its leather with a sigh.
Nothing now will be the same
but neither feels the need for comment –

no banter can add to this moment.
Blind Faith

Francisco Messina, *Pugilatore* (bronze 1929)

A little bull, his legs longing
to spring from the canvas,
slim waist, neck thicker than the thighs
where the gloves rest,
flattened nose, mouth sucking in air.
One eye stares beneath a swollen brow;
the other's defiant:
states that he has won,
will always win,
will never know defeat.

The boxer came back,
approved of the message Messina
had fashioned, showed it to friends
with pride but valued it less
than the next purse –
the coming fight which he won. Of course.

Then ... he met younger opponents,
faced defeat, debt, dictatorship,
war and unwinnable age.
Who he was, what he had once been,
what he had felt was forgotten
– except here.

One eye stares beneath a bronze brow;
the other's defiant:
states that he has won,
will always win,
will never know defeat.

The Apple Tree

With pleasure I'll strip the apple tree
I say, and swing aloft the splintering
tall black ladder, balanced
    sure-handedly.
Like a fireman or jaunty jack I climb

parrying resistance, ignoring the hurt
as she moans to feel my weight.
But I care more for the sodden rungs and
    go up girt
with bags, hooks and blades to come

where her enamelled spoils spreading
beneath are loot to the invader.
But on the exultant heights I
    sense her pleading
for gentleness, for pity, also some

other response. As her tangled hair I part,
as greedily I grasp her firmness,
I'm held by the cidrous scent
    from her heart
and drowsy thoughts check my arm.

On the ladder swaying in proximity
I see no longer the filial Sunday task,
the parental garden with the
    neglected tree
filling a plot bare when I left home.

She tells me of my father's care,
of solicitous sprays, pest-proof bands
of a man and tree relationship
    rich and rare.
She tells of her sorrow to see him harmed

of his gradual blindness she saw before
his human kin and of that bitter day

when his calm, unseeing face she
    scratched sore
-- not out of spite but to raise the alarm.

Mydriasis

No explanation about the eyedrops
just the advice, don't drive
come with a friend.   My friend now
is the tree I seek against
the assaulting enemy above.

A door has been propped open
into a hurricane of light
so a surgeon can probe for signs
of my father's failing.   It's there
but I'm told my field tests are fine.

A tree befriended my father,
scratching his cheek,
alerting us to the tightening grip
on his vision.   The surgeon says
I inherited his inner eye.

Unless watched, the same fist
will seize my sight, blinkering
me from approaching cars,
the bus I now need, neighbours,
the beautiful woman to my left.

The beautiful woman, belladonna,
is the explanation.   In a curtained
room I see mirrored pupils
large as nightshade berries,
the scooped out eyes of a statue.

Five hours, the hurricane passes:
I can face the setting sun.
The belladonna has left the ball.
My father would have loved the pun;

I have touched part of his pain.
Her Hair among Other Things

i.m. Gladys Perman (1911-1986)

She gave me her hair among other things –
silky, sulky hair that clung to my skull
with every passing stab of static
when I wanted an Elvis quiff
to quiver above the girls or flop foppishly.
Unfaithful, fugitive hair. There was always fuzz
on her brush beside the cut-glass toilet set.
She had centre partings, hair nets,
grips at the temple and especially earphones
concealing shapely ears – another
inheritance, like her green eyes
though not her freckles.

I inherited her belief that every penny
you have you earn – though she said
she'd prayed to be able to keep feeding
the shilling-in-the-slot gas meter, but that was
when I was small and she'd lost her next child.
Before the war. Before Hitler became
the why and wherefore of women's work.
She did the post, picked potatoes, fruit, beets
all over Bedfordshire and in the peace
took in homework. To have raked in riches
we (Dad and me included) would have had
to sew seven hundred buttons on card
every evening ... for years. Then there was the baker's
in Barnsbury and the detours I took from school
for a loaf to give the kids their tea –
all tins and farmhouses then, no cut bread
or cobs, let alone ciabatta or bagels. Like her
I had siblings to succour; unlike her they never
held me back. I was her grammar school star
by proxy.

Then Utopia: a New Town. For the first time
she had a house, a bathroom, a garden –

no strangers between her and the earth, no one
to come between her and heaven. And a career
among women she could call friends, working for
Kodak UK in the lost films section: "they'll be easy
to find, dear, they're all of our holiday in Skegness".
She loved the comradeship,
the American paternalism, the perks.
I still have the pictures she took with free films,
frame after frame of family and friends,
some out of focus, most with their heads chopped off –
neatly at the forehead. I shall never know
if they too had fine silky hair.

Fourth World

On a dull day I decide
to attack the wilderness,
shamed by the show
of my neighbour's garden.

Between fruit canes I comb out
the charred skeletons of spring
uncover centipedes and slugs,
thin bleached beetles,
gorged grasshoppers,
a Calcutta of ants as I tug at
an obstinate plantain
and everywhere ladybirds,
glossy leopards in this jungle.

I pile weeds on a bonfire,
look back on the denuded plot
and see stalks standing bare
like a gutted rainforest,
cleared for cultivation
that will never happen –
a fourth world dispossessed,
the gardening impulse over.

Web

October is the spinners' month:
every space and span between shrubs
a finely turned trap for food.
They will work through till November
especially if this weather goes on
until Martin mass, the goose summer.

But it's not fine gossamer that
cocoons my coming: I break a web
across the path and find it binds
hand to trouser, finger to finger.
Hawsers reach to trees
in spires of silk, billowing spinnakers,
mile after mile of strength extruded,
stretched out of their bodies,
like a woman who knits the sinews
of lost love into clothes
for a neighbour's child.

One web catches the sun,
its bowl suspended in seven-foot strands.
It moves in the breeze, glistens
like a coach wheel turning at speed
or a vinyl disk held up to the light
by someone unsure if he wants music.
The breeze blows stronger: it vibrates
in the taffeta sheen of a dancer's skirt
then explodes in stars, haloes and strokes
that only Bridget Riley could reproduce.

At its centre sits its maker,
motionless, a glowing yellow orb,
unaware of the web's beauty,
conscious only of the need
for food.

Red Squirrel

I heard you were here but
never thought to see you
brown against the dark trunk
before you spiralled out of sight.

A long wait then your
curiosity showed the tufted ears
once seen in nursery books
and your brush bright as the
catkins near my face.

I cannot imagine you
cousin to the tree-rat
colonising our country
hauling its skunk tail
over every city park,
snatching what it wants
from picnic rugs.

But you survive and give
hope to all who resist the
new greed which has replaced
your image in children's
minds with cartoon beasts
and burgers – perfect schooling
for the transatlantic rat-race.

Friday Night

Away from the zoom zooming lights
we went homing by the river into the night's
armpit where I offered brave defence
against lions tigers and bears
trampling down a life's fears
of ankle-gnawing rats and stray
horses silent and big as ghouls
but broken branches crackled
did not scuttle and the willows
stood still to let us pass.

Out of the dark lane we came down
to the river where lights from the town
silvered first cloud then still water
with bridges doubled so the reflection
outdid in black the real construction
and we found ourselves walking
along a pop-up card fringed
and feathered with trees – suspended
in a universe of polished pewter
as wide and high as it was deep.

Time followed sense into the abyss
as a lock gate's rearing mass
came nearer across the pewter
water and faint lights appeared
on a thinning barge moored
alongside – lights telling not of
television but living cramped
from birth in a damp dark womb.
Then we came at last to town
and traffic zoomed us back to home.

A Pregnant Bank

Where, like a pillow on a bed,
A pregnant bank swell'd up, to rest
The violet's reclining head,
Sat we two, one another's best.
                    The Ecstasy, John Donne

It's more a bolster than a pillow this particular bank
above the shallow slipping stream where we pause
to rest, and you lie back and quickly fall asleep.

I don't. The sky is too momentous to miss,
a mackerel sky, as they say, a chessboard
of the bolster's scattered swansdown squares.

Bees and birds become quick diagonals
like rooks, bishops – a Boeing in a different
dimension makes a strangely hesitant pawn.

But it's what I feel rather than see
that holds me riveted awake, aware:
below this strong hillock of cooling grass

there are no tunnels, pipes or passages;
this swelling bank was impregnated at a time
when the stream moved mightily moulding

the land like a gouge. Its labour done, the land
was laid out in a lush layette, offering a bosom
for you, my love, to lie upon and rest.

Under Warden Hill

The ancient hill is unchanged, unconcerned
it seems that its apron of fields and farms
was swapped for an ill-sewn suburban
check. It stands out a tombstone to where
Icknield Way lies buried under a crop of
crescents and closes re-emerging only briefly
at Warlud's Bank and Leagrave Marsh – green
blots upon the pristine drabness of suburbia.
We called the hill Wardown like the park
down the road at what was then the town's edge,
downland soaring above greasy smoking streets
coughing up Commer gun carriers, Bedford
trucks, bearings for battleships – Warden/Wardown
in wartime from whose top we could see the track
skirting other hills – Galley, Telegraph, Deacon –
carrying on to Whipsnade in the west.
It's the memory that propels a hot heart-pounding
man upwards past the golfers, up over the sheep
meadow, up though unseeing (sweat fringing his eyelids)
past clumps of candytuft, the occasional orchid
to the summit's proud new prospect: rows of roofs
stewing in their own haze – all the way to Whipsnade.

For a child the sky was wider,
an invitation to dogfight doodles, the downing
of a Dornier in a lush summer orchard
converted to ashen sticks, smelling of baked apple.
Suburbia was still a sketch as if the planner
had tired and gone to play another game.
Roads stopped in hedges, kerb stones
led through plantations of nettles, drains rusted
high and proud above the mud. For six midcentury years
the nation's enemy was nature's friend.

This nature, Warlud's land, and the child made
a pact – the threatened landscape pretending
to be real country safe for a thousand years
making itself fertile where no crops had grown,
thick with flowers in pits and vehicle ruts,

the child running wild through lanes among trees
neither soot-stained planes nor pavement-rooted,
where sensible local children seldom strayed
 – though aged six he'd sat in a sandpit with older boys
smoking Craven A – where adults had become
extinct. A rare stroll down winding Riddy Lane
the soldier centre, wife on one side, child
the other – careless of cars: there were none.
Warlud's land was more his teacher
than the woman with a bun who wrote big
words in chalk while small infants sat
back to back with him and giggled, or
her who taught juniors and rulered his hand
for forming his 'o's with a running loop –
that classroom an abyss in dreaded later dreams
falling, in an endless loop, falling.

Warlud's land taught him the ditches
where violets grew, the bushes with the biggest
berries, the best frogs' spawn found beyond
the sagging barbed wire beside the bridge,
the pollarded ash that made a good ship
sprouting with spears for repelling boarders.
For years they grew unchecked, child and landscape.

The war ended. Even earlier the child had returned
to London to V-1s and V-2s, VE Day, the 11 plus.
With two parents and now a sister, with scrubbed knees,
a blazer and Brylcreamed hair, this was not
a wartime child who could wander unnoticed;
this was a boy competitive as peace always is.
A crowded adolescence replaced the wide skies.
In the three-room flat he was alone only when reading
 – and here his friend Warlud's land returned.
Half-built Grosvenor Road with half-laid road-
way became Casterbridge and here Henchard in stove-
pipe hat sold his wife from a low brick wall
opposite the house of the child's "auntie". At the top
of her garden in a field beyond the fence
they crucified Jesus, they being a centurion and the child
for this was a rubbish dump where few people came

– farther on the road became a sunken track
where the Rogue Male made a hideaway from
murderous Nazi spies (the child would easily have
identified strange adults as Nazis). Lower down
the track joined Riddy Lane where by the bridge
Lenny killed little creatures while John Steinbeck
watched and Ophelia's body floated by – the boy
did not connect the two, reading them at different times.
A high brick wall surrounded Miss Havisham's
house in Nunnery Lane and in the corner shop opposite
Elizabeth Bennet stood fretting in the doorway
waiting for a sight of Darcy. At the top of the lane
was the scout hut, built on brick piles with
a splintered dusty floor, where every
prisoner in every war watched from the window
for a bus to take him into town.

The man sat on the hill recalling the
succesion of images, trying to trace their path
through the streets below. A sudden breeze
from the East Coast en route to Salisbury Plain
made him shiver. He climbed to his feet and walked
gingerly down the slope (the child would run and tumble).
Now he saw the mauve candytuft and orchid,
tried to recapture other settings for other plots
from his other early reading. All he could see
was walls and curtained windows, privet hedges
and Private Residents Only, the same suburbia
through which he would drive for two hours
eighty miles of a late-autumn evening with his
eyes fixed firmly ahead and his imagination
running wild through sunlit lanes among trees
neither garden varieties nor pavement-rooted.

World without Elms

(for Edward Thomas)

I see you surrounded
by great elms, emblems
of an empire already doomed.
You sat on one, felled by a blizzard,
talking with a ploughman passing
with his team. Now no elms grow
tall to be skittles for blizzards.

Others with good reason may mourn
the slash and burn of rainforests;
I lament for the English elm
killed by a foreign canker we
neglected to notice in our frenzy
for free trade in timber.

No longer can eyes hover on
the horizon catching those boughs
billowing like bonfire smoke
above a tall, tapering trunk.
Other trees are noble, even tall;
none matches the melancholy of the elm,
the sad saxophone of the forest,
always close to us – in chairs,
cupboards, coffins – the companion
of our history in these isles.

We receive but what we give

The daffodils don't fill with pleasure,
the blossom is as out of place
as a bridesmaid's dress at a funeral.
Stay on the tarmac is official advice
as we venture for the first time
into the countryside, into what used to be
compensation for our week's weariness,
our leg-stretching landscape, our balm
against people-made injuries – the Eden of
our imagination.

    Stay on the tarmac:
all paths are barred, all farm tracks obstacled
with disinfected straw. Straw's in demand –
the tall trucks ahead dribble down stalks
like sovereigns falling from an over-full purse.
There never was a crisis in which no one
made a killing. A farmer's wife says they
sent their kids away and played opera
on the stereo to shut out the sound of guns.
Somewhere there has to be a cynic (in office
or abattoir) asking what that opera was.

The current concern is foot-and-mouth,
but it could be cow-baiting BSE,
swine fever, pesticide pollution that poisons
streams, makes song birds so scarce that
children will never know a skylark
and what poets were going on about.
Mother earth has supped the poison
her young piled high for the burning;
though this scourge may soon be gone
there's certain to be a returning.
Lady! we receive but what we give
*and in our life alone does Nature live.**

* S.T. Coleridge: *Dejection: an Ode.*

Elegy written in the Hot Weather of July 1995

(After John Scott of Amwell, 1731-1782)

Men are coming to terms with the knees
    they'd suited away for the duration --
it's all shorts, denim, boxer, the shorts
    in which Lord Lugard ruled Africa.

Young women show as much thigh
    as will not get them barred from Tesco's,
Older women wear hats and frocks
    over pressure-cooking underwear.

Sex is in the air, but our sticky
    bodies reject exertion.   Only
butterflies do it, fornicating on the wing,
    a vertical paperchase.

People talk of the hot ... "1990,
    when Barbara's baby was born."
"1976, when we went to Jaywick
    with Jack's Mum".

Political chat has dried up: our
    leaders have gone to exotic
retreats and have less sun than
    their voters.

With global warming, it's all Mediterranean
    now.   No one shops after two,
there are warnings cars cause pollution, with
    no work, we live in the past.

Cafes have tables in the street
    and serve pernod, ouzo and pils.
But the sea is so far away.   And
    we're tired by ten o'clock.

Abney Park Cemetery

Beside the Egyptian portico hieroglyphs
proclaim "The Gates of the Abode
of the Mortal Part of Man".
This was the departure lounge for London's
Dissenters after the gate had closed at Bunhill
Fields – friends who saw them off
festooned it with elms, poplars,
shrubs, a thousand types of rose alone
– alas, all gone.
                    Now everything is draped
in a vast veil of ivy like widows' weeds.
Statues, headstones, blind urns poke
through to show the masons earned their keep.
Angels stand listless and limbless, angels leaning,
angels fallen, angels drunkenly caressing trees
– but talk not of drink in Abney's groves
where Isaac Watts wandered and the tombs
of the Salvation Army's generals stand straight and tall.
"Promoted to Glory" proclaimed in gold paint.

It's hard to fathom one's feelings before
these ranks of Dissidents, Dissenters
standing fast against the establishment
living lives of inordinate restraint
searching for sin at every street corner
battering the world with their bibles
while fighting for freedom and truth:
ministers and missionaries, hymnwriters
humble chapelgoers like Mary Hillum –
she died aged 105 but never travelled by train
or omnibus – a courageous constable
killed by anarchists, deeply mourned infants,
spinsters buried beside puritan parents, like
the Reverend Henry Richard first and only secretary
of the Society for Promoting Permanent
                        and Universal Peace.
That was 1848 the year of revolt when
James Bronterre O'Brien, buried a few yards yonder,
was urging Chartists to demand democracy.

They are restoring Abney, hacking back the creepers
to reveal names, faces unused to the light.
Suckers leave their mark on the angels
like seaweed on the bodies of the drowned.
There were hurricanes here, typhoons of faith,
tempests turning society upside down unseen
by the helmsmen who Sunday by Sunday
stood in their pulpits and promised
a calm voyage to the distant shore.
But Hannah Harcourt of Hoxton knew:

> *Truth must prevail, meanwhile endure*
> *Of worldly peace let others boast.*
> *Amid the storms of life be sure*
> *The noblest spirits suffer most.*

London Nostalgia

Nostalgia for old London
is like a dry onion.
You pick at the skin
and pull away part of another
startlingly white layer.

Covent Garden was once knee-deep
in onions, Spanish or spring,
and shallots squelching under foot.
You peel away the trinkets for tourists,
the cute café society, and find
not costermongers, but poor girls goosed
by Boswell and Pepys, beggars with babies
in Inigo Jones's baroque portico,

and in layers beneath, aged nuns
growing shallots in the convent dirt.
Nostalgia in London is digging
for the dirt that once spawned
onions smooth and green.

Highbury Corner

It's not easy to make out the corner
at Highbury Corner, since there's now
a roundabout, built where a bomb bit
into the Christmas cake of Compton Terrace.

No modern child would dare plunge
into that stampede, as I did daily in one
direction or another, running always late
for school or choir reached via the Northern Line
-- a branch of the branch line now closed --
the Fields for swimming or Saturday flicks.

Then Upper Street was a mighty river
of furrowed tramlines, choppy with tar bricks
surging like a great wave at Highbury Corner
as clanging frigate trams, swaying inwards
and 609 and 611 trolley buses
like tugboats, grunt-hiss purring onwards
reached the calm waters of Holloway Road.

Who now here could stand and stare
-- as an occasionally not-quite-late boy did –
at winkle and whelk stalls, blue plaques where
writers had lived, a bishop in a purple
cassock, and the weekly outings of Quentin Crisp,
out turkey-strutting with bright rouged lips?

The Grinling Neighbourhood

After the notice to visitors in Mandarin
and Vietnamese ... *vàn phông thông bào* ...
the name is a surprise: the Grinling Gibbons
Primary School. But this is Deptford,
where the Dutch-born Grinling – asylum-seeker,
economic migrant? – was found chiselling by John
the Diarist Evelyn, ever on the look-out for talent,
and introduced to Royalty and Wren.

Once free of damp Deptford, Grinling
was never again to be a common carver.
In St. Paul's and Petworth, Piccadilly and Blenheim
he fashioned foliage and fruit, leaves, linnets and lute-
strings to cascade down parlour walls and choir-stalls
– arpeggios of sensuality – made the baroque
stand out in three exquisite dimensions. His Venetian
lace cravat – lovingly cut in limewood –
was actually worn by Horace Walpole.

In Deptford, squeezed between the coiling
Thames and congested New Cross,
the Grinling school is not great architecture,
a mere hut complex of sixties building – but
here in obscurity may work masters of future style
and fame, asylum seekers' kids with skills
unknown or forgotten within these shores. Is
there still an Evelyn to discover them?

Real and imagined – Cockington, South Devon

The usual route to the thatched village
is through watermeadows reclaimed from scrub –
as colonies of rosebay willowherb confirm.
The path in places is planked with pine
wire-meshed so that sandals cannot slip;
at interesting intervals wildlife ponds
are set symmetrically in the stream.

The other way is longer, lonely
dark even on the brightest day:
it begins behind a gasworks
continues into muddy Scadson Wood
where twin ditches each with a stream
mark an ancient parish boundary.
There's a certain magic in the droplets

of light, more in the growing sense
that the ditch-pairing is a twilight trick
the reflection in a wall of glass
that cannot mirror you the intruder
until you have been here a hundred years.
Somewhere beyond the second stream
branch shadows are forming the shapes

of people who lived in Cockington
before it was thatched, unthatched
and thatched again.

St George's Ivychurch

The longest nave on Romney Marsh
says the guide and almost as wide
with the aisle idly added by some lord.
Rot now inhabits this expanse
though hidden behind dusty plastic screens.
Outside lichen blooms on every wall
and headstones stoop towards five
small mounds swaddled in moss.

In faint chalk on a blackboard
the churchwardens ask for donations
and we give – a coin drops
into the empty padlocked box.
But should we?   The dozen
hedged bungalows and double row
of council houses can never fill
this expanse even if some
revivalist priest rivalled their TV

The many churches on the marsh
are chequers on a board of intensely
farmed fields serving only hikers
and retired judges out for a drive.
Give back this plot to the marsh
elsewhere drained and drilled for wheat!
Let the roof fall in, nettles invade
the nave, let God's old garland
of ivy reclaim its heritage!

I pace uneven floors planning
where stones must fall, briars
branch out, mosses multiply
and come across a coffee jar
containing fresh sprigs of mallow
and a card written in school crayon:
For St George's from Jemma and Jan.
Unknown names, but their crayon
could replace rafters, repel
vegetation, send a cynic on his way.

Corked

They work in pairs moving methodically
among the chocolate trunks, choosing
which to incise with their curved axes.
Gently, the skill of generations,
they prise away treasured slabs,
drop them into the long grass and on
the golden waistcoat of inner bark
paint the final digit of the year – not
to be disturbed for nine years when
the furry fabric will grow again turning
from beige through Dao-wine red to brown,
a gestation for the wine's stopper longer
than for the liquor or its drinker.

Thus is born nature's own bung, the cork
of our culture, popping appropriately
for life's feasts, a corker to amaze us,
burnt to darken actors' faces, the
yielding door to evenings of pleasure,
breaking sometimes in impatient hands
but able to be squeezed back for more later
(except for champagne) – known to the Romans
named *alcorque* by the Moors (not then
tee-total), the bark of the cleverest tree
in the garden of Eden that learned
from the serpent to shed its skin and live.

The pair drag the bark to their truck
reckoning the price in escudos for they are
Portugal's poorest, cork-farmers of the Alentejo.
Far away in the wineries of Safeway and M&S
they are promoting the plastic stopper, a strategic
move in the carbons of convenience – not just
oblivious to Portuguese plight but prepared
to bury them with PR speak. We are saving cork
trees from being cut down, says a bulletin from Marks
and the future of the Alentejo's cork oaks
is flattened by a plastic bullet and PR speak.

Monemvasia, Peloponnese

The Gibraltar of the Aegean
a rock to shelter against, for enemies
to bruise their fists against, a rock
to challenge the climber. From a high
stone wall proud of my summitry

I look down on the church most tourists
aspire to – waiting for cloud shadows
to pass and the dome to be lit against the sea
like a bow light – breakers prancing
to starboard, chiselled smoothness to port.

In the micro world of my wall Nature
applies grasses and weals of pink lichen
to pretend the rock's bloody history
is only a trick of the light.
But beckoning ants draw my eye

under the lichen to a red line
a roof tile, sharp as a sword cut.
Who climbed up here tiles
on his back, to build or rebuild and
mortared that tile between the stones?

It's not the ascent that worries me,
what goes up ... no, *whoever* goes up
to enjoy the view to spy out enemies
to feel superior over ants that cannot
climb so well, eventually must go down.

Who was the mortarer, how did he descend?
Was he a Frank never happy here alive
wrapped in pigskin when dead, or a Turk
hurled from the cliff by Greek patriots
or a Venetian skuttling to his ship?

It was blood that flowed not lichen
and rock catching the evening sun.

Ancient mortarer, may you have
have descended slowly, lit like me
by the evening sun thinking of wine,
a woman's company at a candlelit
table by the sea.

A Day in Greece

Grey mullet chasing through the shallows
flip silver side up as our long shadows
reach out from the sand. And the sun too
retreats, draping Byron's sweeping mountains
in the muslin of boarding-house windows.

In the market, tomatoes large as melons,
damp stacks of beetroot, chillies cheekily
curling, wine-glazed eggplants had laughed
at our wonder. Then Nemea grapes
piled high, blue blushed. We'd raised a fistful.
How much? *Tipota, ena doro* -- nothing a gift.

Surprised, grateful as much for their grins,
we'd bought and bought till our arms hung
heavy with fruit and our minds
strained at exchange rates to find
how little we'd paid. How do they make
a living? Low expectations was no answer.

Singapore

for my father

We were five minutes late landing,
problem with winds over the Bay of Bengal.
You had wind of the atom bomb but landed
not knowing if the Japs had surrendered.

I'm walking through your past and our future.
Cranes construct towers between every
tree root, stern Asian faces do billion
dollar deals and everywhere is clean.
By order. You couldn't drop a fag end now
as you came ashore or risk a $500 dollar fine.
The same penalty for urinating in a lift or
chewing gum – not that you'd have done either.

In Raffles litter is permitted: yuppies
happy on gin-slings at $35 a time
threw monkey nut shells on the floor,
I looked hard but couldn't
see your ghost searching for your friend
Albert down from the Burma railway.

They call this a tiger economy, more
intoxicating than their tiger beer.
They're now giving the beast an imperial past:
"Give the future of your business a glorious
past" says the hoarding. What was glorious
was that you couldn't wait to get home
and vote against the British Empire!

Raffles Hotel

Takeo Bukoshita and Tokyo banking colleagues
had a buffet high tea in the Raffles Hotel
billiard room, eating yam dumplings, smoked salmon,
Chinese eggs, samosas, steamed lotus seed buns,
fresh strawberries, chocolate cheesecake,
lychees and drank Lipton's tea,
all competing to pay by credit card.

Brian Butterworth and backpacking friends
sat nearby, eating cucumber sandwiches,
smoked salmon canapés, ham quiche, cheese
straws, crème brulée, apricot cheesecake,
kiwi tarts, melon (both galla and water),
fresh cherries, fresh strawberries, lemon soufflé
and scones with raspberry jam and clotted cream,
washing it down with Earl Grey tea, and
only just scraped together the $30 apiece bill.

As a colonel, Takeo's boss's grandfather drank
in Raffles twice a week in '42 and '43.
Brian's great-uncle was there for a week in '45
after his release from the Burma-Siam railway.

So who won the war?

Which war are we talking about?

Who cares?

GARDENS IN TOKYO

1. *Kiyosumi*

Cursive syllables
cut in the rock: "the frog leaps,
the sound of water".

Smiling small women pace
gravel paths, seeking
Basho's blessing before
sitting down to lunch;
silver pencils held in new
leather caress haiku strokes
away from traffic noise,
financial crisis, commuters
competing to crowd
in subway cars.

> Smooth stepping stones line
> the pool's edge: ducks on water
> like pebbles on ice.

Driver Daimatsu bored
with waiting buys popcorn
casts it on the water: at first
incredulous ducks gather
joined by gulls garnered
on an avian internet;
an egret disgusted at such
gusto strides away
on thin yellow legs.

> Market forces find
> a garden: birds fight for food
> the sound of water.

2. Kitanomaru Park

Bonzai, bushido – kimono, kamikazi –
useful words for the visitor says the book.

I'm similarly in two minds coming
from the crowds which waved
paper flags at the Emperor's appearance.
Crows are in the pines. At the gate
families greet each other with bows, 2
light cigarettes and gossip,
their children play tag, pull faces,
poke out their tongues then giggle
as the pink-faced *gaijin* passes.

Bonzai, bushido – kimono, kamikazi –
useful words for the visitor says the book.

Black windowed buses line the road
the crude outline of all Japan's islands
in white paint with slogans sinister
in their extent. The Rising Sun
flag flutters from bull bars.
A jack-booted man with swastika
armband passes unseeing policemen.
Crows are in the pines.

Bonzai, bushido – kimono, kamikazi –
useful words for the visitor says the book.

By the fountains a man props his bicycle
against a tree, sits and takes out bread.
Crows come down from the trees
swooping and squawking; pigeons
gather to gobble the man's scraps
with quiet, orderly greed. The crows
keep their distance pecking each other
croaking frustration. Is this
the natural order? Will the crows
in time come to the front?

Bonzai, bushido – kimono, kamikazi –
useful words for the visitor says the book.

3. *Hama-rikyu*

A garden as old as the shoguns,
shorn to perfection, difficult to approach –
a skywalk across expressways or
you dodge juggernauts at the Tokyo
wholesale market.　It's raining:
I'm alone on new-raked gravel.

A heron rises from the reed-walls
of an imperial duck-shoot, skirts
symmetrical pines, flies seawards
under the muslined harbour bridge.
A lone machine dispenses
sweet coffee in hot slim cans.

From a log shelter I attempt a sketch.
The tidal pool is in no mood
for reflection.　Planked bridge built
Kyoto style and teahouse sit
on a surface of corrugated card.
The mist lifts like a theatre trick
and skyscrapers stare down.

I lack the artist's eye to filter
culture from capital, feudal
heritage from Forties horrors.
A wizened couple come near,
gesture their wish for me to snap
them with green cardboard Fujimatic.
Toothy thanks, grins, a raised hand
to show how tall the foreigner seems.
The tidal pool resumes reflecting –
timber, trees, towering office blocks.

The Wasted Years

by T.S. Hellavalot

Bovril makes the cruellest lunch, breeding
Lymphocytes from dead lambs, mixing
Rumour and science, stirring
Dull Gummer to righteous pain.
Winter gave us 'flu, feeding
GPs' pockets with attendance fees.
Summer surprised us, coming up with the first BSE
In a shower of headlines, we stopped
Eating meat, calves' hoof jelly,
And drank lager, like the Germans:
Kein englisch Fleisch, spracht Helmut,
                        Vörsung durch Technik.
And when our children were straying into McDonald's
We took them out quickly, to the street,
And we were frightened. We said, Mc-spew,
Mc-spew it quick. And up it came.
In the veggie-bar, there you feel free.
I retched much of the night, and had bizimuth
                      in the morning.

Where are the microbes that clutch, what horrors grow
Out of this Tory rubbish?   Son of Thatcher,
You cannot say, or guess, for you know only
A heap of broken promises, where the City grins
And the NHS gives no shelter, cricket scores no relief,
Privatisation no clean water.   Only
There is hope under this red flag
(Come and vote New Labour under this red flag)
And I will show you something different from either
The unemployed at morning rising to no hope
Or the homeless at evening preparing cardboard beds.
I will show you fear in the capitalist lust

   Frisch weht T. Blair
   Der Europ zu,
   Mein Irisch Herr
   Paisley ist Kuh.

'You gave me the Lottery first a year ago;
'They called me the Lottery girl.'
-- Yet when we came back, late, from the Lottery payout,
Your bank account full, your tee-shirt wet, I could not
Speak, and my brakes failed, I was neither
Living nor dead, and I knew nothing,
Looking into the surgeon's light, the silence.
Ertrinken im Major's Meer.

The Man from Perth

I met him in Perth – the other Perth
"the one where they waste their money!"
He was overdressed and clearly distressed
for the day was hot and sunny.

I thought it cool to be by the pool
where the bar served juice and goodies,
but then he said he'd "rather be dead
than gape at young girlies' bodies!"

So we took a trip on a tourist ship
to a wine lodge up the river
where he asked for tea or alcohol-free
drink. "Or wine, sir?" "Never!"

I went by coach to a famous beach
where the dolphins come to your call
but he said he'd been and found the scene
"just miles and miles of bugger all!"

Scrap-Iron Words (2014)

Distant Copse

On a normal morning no one would see it
with parcel vans, trucks, four wheel-drives
whirling around the elevated way like a discus-
thrower winding up, ready to be hurled
                                    on to the motorway.

He saw it first when he was late, a Tuesday,
descending behind a Tesco truck, allowing his eyes
to wander to the left – a stand of timber fringeing a hill.
It stayed with him all day, flashing like an emergency exit
during speeches, overrun agendas, routine reports –
a copse on the horizon – a cock's comb catching the sun.

It would be a wood that filtered out all noise, that
gave shelter from the north wind, a wood where aconites
bluebells anemones grew, from the far side of which
you could see the sea. He debated whether to use
a day off to find it, explore it, make it
his own for all time, but he knew he never would.

No road would go there, he would twist and turn
trying to keep the copse ahead, find it moving to his rear
while he was bogged in traffic, road works, dead end
estates of burned out cars. It was better to keep it as
a remembered promise, somewhere on the edge,
a distant copse catching the sun, a part of his private
iconostasis – like a Schubert theme
or a fellow-creature's smile.

Carless

Someone's bound to stop for you, she said
but cars came by in anxious convoy
watching each other scarcely catching
sight of the walker who at least
could stop and look
at cows, curving hills, postcard cottages
and Dartmoor distant over the hedge,

at vetch, tall agrimony, old man's
beard beneath – there's fifty species
a square metre, if you count the grasses –
and purple knapweed which John Clare
said girls would strip and nurse in their bosoms to see
if they would marry the boy of their choice
if the pod blossomed again.

Clare walked across three counties
to home in that carless careless age
when every child walked to school,
unwillingly or otherwise,
when leg-strong labourers left hours early
as they still do in countless car-scarce
countries of the other world.

Our past, their present.
But whose future?

The Patience of the Crocuses

It's been the coldest March, the snowiest Easter,
the longest winter in living memory.
It's not what we've come to expect
from modern weather. So what if it
was worse in 1983, in forty-seven, in seventeen?
Given global warming what we want is –
well – warmth.

Men complained, Nature coped.
For weeks on end daffodils stood stiff
with scarce a sneak of yellow.
The patience of the crocuses, wrapped
in their tight spears. Apples which in
other years would have become
a joyous spring mulch, now sit proudly,
coldly firm in their hanging plastic bags.

Is it only we humans who are impatient,
flying off for the sun – probably finding rain?
In Wales they've suspended the law against livestock
burials. Thousands of lambs, ewes, calves
perished in the snow – ewes gave birth
under six-foot drifts. Could they not have waited?
Of course not: birth and death don't wait.
Or was it us to blame with our greedy deadlines
for spring lamb?

Impatience is our modern watchword:
tailgating, short-cuts, jostling, speed-dating,
must-haves, must-dos, must-sees –
don't wait, phone now.
But it's also what quickened the pace
of change, that sped on the French Revolution,
the Industrial Revolution, in fact all revolutions.
That created instant internet access,
faster communications. Faster everything.

Evolution was built on patience
but it's speeding up, we're told.

If there's a question of men and women
imitating the patience of the crocuses,
or of spring flowers learning, being
programmed, or just developing
an ability to open on time –
whatever the weather –
I know which it will be. Or
I think I do.

Rivers Nursery, Sawbridgeworth

An orchard under a flightpath
of perilous arrivals, every four
minutes – no more, no less
for therein lies loss.

But the trees
are wiser, have revised
their checkerboard ranks
with young next to old next to
older next to sprawling
next to saplings.
So blossom does not arrive
all at once to be caught
in the deadly flightpath of frost.

Thistles on Widbury

The thistles are a surprise
after the blocks of growth-regulated
wheat and ripening brown rape –
a hillside wholly of thistles, spaced
generously like middle-class housing
to give room for ragwort and teasels,
food for peacocks and fritillaries.

I've read Lorrain and other landscape
painters made them foreground features
but not these thistles – proud, bristling.
I stand transfixed until you say you
hear a skylark and I look up,
searching among the swallows and
clouds of my own floaters for a sight
of the bird that fires off notes faster
than any instrument of music or war.
I heard one first on a firing
range in the silence from sten guns.

The Danes took war down from Widbury
and terrorised the small town by
the river below. Somewhere under
the corn lies their camp, now only
crop marks seen by the skylark.
But the town has grown and crowds
the valley as thistles never could,
sprouting steel tubes and towers
among older orange roofs and the
cowls of redundant malt kilns
turned inward like broken limbs.

We descend by a path steep enough
to cleanse the brain of contrasts
and enter the valley of the Ash,
lush with growth from summer rains.
We came here before and you
saw a kingfisher dart down the river.

Now reeds, sedge and willows spread
over the wine-coloured water,
providing privacy for lives below.
This is Nature as it's painted –
concealing, urging us to forget.

Blame

Incident near Djakovica in Kosovo, 14 April 1999

It's a funny schoolyard word
to use – not who was responsible?
The medal-breasted general said
all his men acted responsibly –
a tape by the pilot was played
of how he made several passes
over the vehicles getting (he said)
a close look with his eyeballs
and infra-red targetting pod;
quite satisfied they were military
he then laser-bombed the lead
vehicle, which was a tractored trailer
refugee-crowded with their load
of mattresses – poor possessions –
scattered, burned, everywhere blood.
It's not who we can accuse
just where to pin blame instead:
the pilot, the general, Nato powers,
the Serbian president safe in bed,
or warfare, history, even God?
Perhaps it's best to blame the pod.

Dream Park

A wound in the heart of Manhattan
measuring half a mile for muggers
by two miles of mayhem
in this world's murder capital,
eight hundred junkie-hiked acres
celebrated in films and broadcasts,
the butt of every news editor
without a story – for there is always
a serial killer, rapist, big cat,
reptile, mystery virus at large
in Central Park.
                     Central surprise!
Watercolourists squat under the elms
aspiring to be Monets or at least
Jackson Pollocks,
nannies chatter in an oakglade
as if in Kensington Gardens –
there's no Peter Pan but they do have Alice
and a Hans Christian Anderson –
joggers, rollerbladers who'd love to fly,
picnickers and Shakespeareans
all totally colour blind,
a lumpy brown bird with a smudge of orange
that goes by the name of a robin,
the flamboyant cardinal (a sop to the Irish),
land-locked cormorants and egrets,
rabbits, timid squirrels far less grisly grey
than the export version –
within these rolling acres
New Yorkers can anchor their dreams –
dreams that went undeclared at Immigration
or Ellis Island, dreams whose archetypes
we recognise here but never could
in Denver or Hollywood,
dreams that go to the heart
of a highly cultured culture-denying city.

On a baseball diamond in the Great Lawn
an old man in old long-johns

grasps a bat to his shoulder and swings
at the empty field.   Dusk descends.
Hours later he is still swinging
at distant towers –
swinging and dreaming.

Normal

We crave it only when we've lost it
when we're desperate for what we assumed,
consumed and took for granted.
The silence of the guns, a decent meal,

the smile of the lover who came back,
the lost child in its mother's arms,
after the cyclone a leaf spiralling down
and caught in a spider's thread.

Intentionally Homeless

The adviser – let's call her Sue – could feel
a migraine coming on. It was not the fault surely
of the woman before her, clean, a little shabby,
clearly worried, shuffling listlessly through
her documents – from the eviction notice backwards.

No, Sue recognised the type. They were coming
in increasing numbers. No, it could have been the telly
she'd watched at breakfast –
the minister Mr S.O. Sincerely – explaining the new
benefits cap, how it will help the poor. In the long run.
How they can't look for work because of their benefits,
how capping benefits brings them to the level where one
can say: Look, from this point onwards you can always
afford to look for work. He flashed a smile, his bald head
caught the light and Sue felt pain.

The client said she had looked for work, did eighteen
hours a week cleaning. Couldn't work more because
of the children. As she was working, she no longer
claimed housing benefit – just as the minister said.
And as she no longer claimed benefit, she stopped
paying the rent. Now she faced eviction .. Friday ..
five days away after 12 years in the house.

Sue took the docs, noting the figures on her laptop
as she made two piles – one for income, the other for
demands – rent .. council tax .. uilities ..TV licence ..
television rental .. credit cards .. court fines .. doorstep
lenders. The laptop totted up hundreds, thousands –
a fortune if there hadn't been a minus sign in front.
The client had been to the council for help. They refused
help because – by not paying the rent she and her
husband had made themselves *"intentionally homeless"*.

"Intentionally homeless" made the client cry. "We didn't
mean to ..." she began but Sue's migraine blanked out the
rest. Earlier she had looked at the regulations:

"The council should look at the whole of your circumstances in deciding whether you deliberately did or didn't do something. It may decide that you deliberately did or didn't do something that caused you to become homeless if:

- *point   you didn't pay the rent or mortgage when you could have afforded to*
- *point   you were evicted for antisocial behaviour*
- *point   you left accommodation that you could have stayed in.*

If you got into rent arrears or mortgage arrears because of genuine financial difficulties that were beyond your control, the council should not consider you to be intentionally homeless."

But they did. This was when Sue's migraine got worse, when the flashing lights took a tight grip on her vision, producing a central blankness she could not see beyond.

Maggie Merilyn

She is hair – not has, *is* hair.
Think back to before silkiness,
conditioning, streaking, bubble
cuts, perms and waves ... think Rapunzel
if you must, but more down to earth.
She circles the supermarket concentrically,
puffing as she pushes an empty trolley,
muttering as she remembers what she's
forgotten, will probably again forget.
A model for charity shop fashions –
the polka-dot dress, cardigan and
belted coat her mother would have thought
outmoded. When she was fifteen she
was the town joke, the sort that boys
snatched a kiss from, grabbed her tits,
the sort most girls wanted to protect.
It was then that a wag gave her the name
Maggie Merilyn – throw no stones!
She's remained Maggie as a result.
On the trolley her hands sit red and hard,
broken nails and cracked knuckles: they mean
that she's a cleaner, someone everyone calls on
to scrub those steps, that outside toilet.
But her hidden meaning is she's a carer,
has a Mam or maybe a man waiting
at home somewhere, someone to talk to,
maybe with, a saviour from pointlessness,
someone she lets her hair down for,
using it to wipe the feet
she's washed with her tears.

Meeting at Mortschach

They sat opposite each other outside
the *hof*, she facing the mountain,
he the valley. For hours since he arrived
they'd walked and talked, now was a time
for holding still the acknowledged present.
She screwed her eyes against the sun,
lake blue eyes he remembered – the spot
on her cheek that always worried her.

It was a month since she'd told him
casually at the book fair in a corner
about her new friend. She had thought
he would shrug his shoulders sheepishly,
say: well, good luck. It had been years
in any case; and he now drank. He had thought
maybe the friend was a plant, <u>they</u> had never
forgiven him for publishing her in the black
party days, <u>they</u> were still strong even after
the wall came down. She told him. They parted.
Then he sent her poems, passionate playful poems,
in English which was not the first language
of either of them. Maybe her emails were read,
but his poems were not encrypted as once
his letters were, just straight in a line to her soul.

They absorbed these things; the sun went
behind the mountain. Come and help me pack,
she said. Inside she moved the suitcase from the bed
and clung to him, close, tight, safe, silent until
the car came to take her to Innsbruck.

Through Train

He'd always sat facing, eager to look
ahead – the next stop, fresh farms, villages,
glimpses of the engine on a bend,
forging forward. As a child
he'd imagine a white horse racing
the train, leaping hedges,
soaring Chagall-like over church steeples.

He had always been excited at travelling
by train: those ancient steamers stuttering
up the foothills of the Hartz Mountains,
the express he used to take to Leipzig when
he worked for Weimar,
the carefully not-an-express on which
he escaped in thirty-eight.
Trains excited him. Their economy was his life.

He knew there were other coaches behind
crowded with families, children,
noise, even an observation car for colonels
and canons nostalgic to look back.
But he had to work. There were notes
and an agenda for the planning meeting
he was rushing towards, planning a future –
tearing him away from the view.

The work absorbed him, the landscape
was less dramatic. He must have
fallen asleep for when he awoke
it was dark, he was cold and alone
in that part of the train.
He looked round, saw people
crowding about a door.
No observation car. Just a door.

He felt drawn towards it, to look back
at what they were looking at, perhaps to see
if there was someone he'd recognise.
Others were gathering at the door:

he knew he had to decide.
It was a challenge.
Would he go or would he be one
of the few still looking ahead in this –
the last carriage?

Hand in the Water

Count me out on classical oblations,
hands cupped so close that the palms
shine white under captured water –
that soon finds a fissure between fingers
and drains away, dribbling and dripping
from helpless elbows. And not for me
the one-handed cupping of Gideon's gang
– too little, too many scoops – I'd die
of thirst or fatigue or fall on my knees
crouching and slurping with the crowd.

Yet leave water in its element and my hand
itches to play – to splash like a child,
make waves flick foam, to dangle
and dabble, trail fingers over the side
of a boat with a hint of fear that they're
bait (will be bit) or part the waters
with one's arms whether walking or afloat
or thrust a fist into a torrent to feel its power.
Hand in the water – yes: water in the hand – no!

Queue

It was a queue like no other queue under
the sun – or the moon or artificial lighting –
a queue apparently not for anything, not to anywhere,
just a queue.

I joined the queue behind a man with large ears
holding the arm of a thin woman in a hat.
Behind me, I noticed, were children but they
were soon gone.

Nobody stayed in their place in the queue,
it was all change all the time and yet there
was no jostling, no juggling or queue jumping –
just the queue.

We queued with right shoulders right up
against a wall – then the next wall at right
angles, through a doorway and back along
the back of the wall.

Room after room of walls, of queues.
Through other doors came other queues
moving back from where we had come,
retro queues (so to speak).

A line of shuffling folk just like us
though as they passed it was just possible
to see their clothes were not really
like our clothes.

No one spoke while queuing, all we could
have spoken to were backs of heads and backs.
Then we stopped. People looked around.
Still no one spoke.

Not then, not until someone sneezed with
the dust, someone else sat down and people
began to smile, to laugh and chat – about
nothing in particular.

Only slowly did content come as people spoke of
the colour of the walls, the pattern on the floor,
the style of their shoes and ... where did you buy
those stylish jeans?

Someone in the doorway tried speaking to a man
from the opposite queue. But that was awkward.
It made other queuers stop what they were doing
and stare.

So through the night. Some sank down and slept,
others leaned, many continued talking.
Relationships were formed, food was found even
for a feast.

It felt good, a real relief after the queuing.
Then came the voice from above: "Can I
have your attention please. Can I have your
attention please.

"All offers and availability have now expired.
I repeat: all offers and availability have now
expired. However ... new offers are available
for queuers.

"If you wish to take advantage of these
then form a queue against the left-hand wall.
Form a queue against the left-hand wall.
Those not wishing

"to queue for new offers, should form a queue
for the exit – against the right-hand wall.
Offers: left-hand wall, exit: right-hand wall.
End of announcement."

We queued with right- or left-hand shoulders
against the left or right wall – And no one spoke.
It was the end to comradeship, relaxation,
queuing again

apparently not for anything, not to anywhere,
or at least we were queuing for offers
we could not appreciate until and if
we received them

or queuing to get to the exit,
queuing to stop queuing in fact.
And no one spoke – for all we could have spoken to
were the backs of heads or backs.

Proof

I had forgotten it was written
till with a splat it hit the mat:
I tear it from its cover, and read,
read there and then the most fascinating
book in the world – my life condensed
in one volume. Delight to see myself in print
soon fades, becomes dismay, bewilderment:
why are all my I's changed to he except
for a few in double quotes ... and that part
where I was philosophical and private
now refers to "the singular first person singular".
Why the American usage, why criticism that
I lacked life goals, spurned relationships?
Some editor has excised my best moments –
when I was in love and loved, when I felt free,
close to creation – all relegated to an appendix
of reported speech. And why the interpolations –
things I omitted as too trivial, or tricky,
now all there with things I don't remember at all,
that surely couldn't have happened.
I look for clues among the acknowledgements,
finds names I'd forgotten or tried to forget,
names I never knew, would rather never have known.
The brown paper cover says "Allegedly a Life
(a Provisional Title)" close brackets. Comment
is allowed on one side of a sheet of A4. I'm instructed
to send it back at my own expense.
No publication date but there is a deadline:
to be returned before the end of .... last month.

Grandeur and Greatness

i.m. Juliet Bingley (1925-2005)

Some saw you as grand
but you reserved your pride for grandchildren
– who won prizes, tottered in grown-ups' shoes,
chased through your orchard like a pride of lions –
and for grandparents who played their part in empire
though you sailed out of Valetta harbour
proud of that island's independence.

But of course you had grandeur –
the Admiral's consort who cared about
the kids of those below decks, the hospital
almoner punctually catching the early bus
to St. Marks. St. Mark's followed Malta
then there was MIND and your MBE.
How magnificent your 'M' years were.

But what made you great was your clear
acute, compassionate eye. I see you waiting
for a train on a derelict platform deep among
rounded hills, having noted where the catkins and
bluebells bloomed, or warming to a motherly
moorhen as much as to a woman munching a bun
as you inevitably will to sprawling beggars
and their dogs on the King's Cross concourse.

There may not be grandeur in your verse but
it has a great flavour of the great life you lived.

Requiem

for Anna Akhmatova

I saw you in a room in the Randolph Hotel,
sitting still as stone against the light.
The photographer made me hold his gear
while he manoeuvred you for a portrait
to illustrate why the University of Oxford
would dub you with an honorary degree.

To me you were a name and more, a memory
of a tall cross-legged woman in blue,
painted before the revolution, carelessly letting
your ochre wrap fall to the dual-tone floor.
Later I learned you'd loved Modigliani,
been the toast of Petrograd, been wooed

repeatedly by Pasternak, and stayed in newly-named
Leningrad behind bolted doors while terror
marched incessantly on the banks of the Neva.
But you went on believing in Russia, in Resurrection.
It was Stalin himself who turned you to stone;
his henchmen called you a harlot and a nun.

I wanted to see that woman in blue
in the muffled figure in that hotel room:
the Roman nose was there but not the fine
shoulder-blades stretching your blue-white skin.
I wanted you to smile but you had said
the glad ones that smiled were the dead.

Rosie

i.m. Eleanor Irene Redgrave MBE

They had put her by the window
in a winged, high-back chair which
swallowed her bird-like form.
She was in woollens, right for the time of year
but quite foreign to the silks she always
wore under her Church Army duffle coat.
He remembered the chuck wagon where
the platoon came for tea and wagon wheels,
her humour and the fact that she was a better
commander of men than he could ever be.

'Irene, you've got a visitor,' said the nurse.
The figure in the armchair was somewhere else.
'Just sit beside her and hold her hand. That's
best.' He sat close and touched her arm.
He spoke the name by which the whole
Rhine Army knew her – 'Rosie'. Still no
recognition. Then he remembered that raucous
song the Royal Scots had sung for her – which
sparked a military row since they'd chorused it under
her window after entering the garrison at 3 a.m.

'Darling Flo, I love you so,' he whispered
with the semblance of a tune, hoping for a response
before he got to the bit where the moonlight
flits across her ... The head turned slightly,
there was the hint of a smile on her Blitz-damaged
face. He told her how wonderful it was to see her,
how the weather was colder but wet. The smile
lingered but she was somewhere else. He told her
Lady Chatterley's Lover was now legal and
they were ending National Service. So they
sat while he prattled on about the world at large
and she lapsed into the dream from which only
loud-mouthed young soldiers seemingly
could rouse her.

Thrown Away

"Afghan throw blankets and throw rugs, originally named because the materials used would decay and the items would be thrown away, were first made in Afghanistan and commonly included geometric designs and many holes in the pattern."

"Captain Thomas Chuck Collins ... killed at Gundamuck in the disastrous campaign of Afghanistan January 13th 1842 in the 41st year of his age."   Memorial in St. Mary's Church, Ware

Did Susannah Collins know how?
  Yes, Dr. Bryden, sole survivor of the retreat from Kabul
  – a Scot of few words – made a detour to tell her.
  So Susannah knew (as the poet said) he had gone
  to his death like a soldier.
Did she know when?
  Bryden told her the date. She put it on the memorial.
Did she know why?
  They said it was to defend India, Jewel in the Imperial
  Crown, though in her heart she doubted how that could
  be.

All Luydmila knew was that Grisha was one of thousands
– the Kremlin said fewer than fifteen, others said fifty.
Did she know how?
  No, the bodies were brought to the Kazansky station
  periodically, after midnight. All she was told was where
  and when to collect it.
Did she know when?
  No, all the bodies had were names and numbers.
Did she know why?
  They said it was to support their Marxist brothers in
  Kabul – families were encouraged to say that. But
  the Committee of Soldiers' Mothers said that was shit.
  Gorbachev agreed and brought home Russia's sons.

Sally went to Wootton Bassett to meet Brian –
borne from the plane on six sergeants' shoulders.
Did she know how?
  It was an explosive device. The MoD sent an officer
  to tell her before it was announced on the BBC.

Did she know when?
   Oh yes, she was given all the details.
Did she know why?
   The Prime Minister said it was to keep Britain's
   streets safe from terrorists, the officer said it
   was his devotion to duty as a soldier,
   but she preferred to think he was helping a comrade.

Amina actually saw her son Abdi being killed.
Did she know how?
   Yes, he was in the house with the older men
   when the missile from a drone devastated the district.
Did she know when?
   Yes, of course – she was returning from the fields.
Did she know why?
   Maybe Abdi went to the wrong house,
   maybe he wanted to be a soldier like the Taliban
   though he preferred geography to jihad.
   Does a mother ever know why?

Morning

I ran beside our river today in that bright
hour between a shower and its shadow
passed a couple stepping gingerly through puddles
disturbed a mallard and its mate
and was surprised by the resurrection
of the earth, the quick growth of grasses
the yellow spears thrusting above willows
and wondered if it was the same with you
if you were running by your canal
and if I could encapsulate my picture
send it signed with a kiss by cygnet express
so it could reach you before clouds sent
the sun scudding for shelter.

A Forgotten Meeting

(James Cameron and Albert Schweitzer, 1953)

It was a meeting of two Greats –
of that there is no doubt.
A Nobel Peace Prize winner, a saint
in his own lifetime, sought out
by a famous journalist who'd travelled four
thousand miles to ... To do what? To genuflect
like a pilgrim? – obviously not! To observe and report
like a good reporter? Or was Cameron in some respect
a beast from the Fleet Street jungle,
ready to rip apart Schweitzer's saintliness
and leave the bones for others to pick over
in the yellowing pages of the popular press?

Whatever his motives, the fact is
Cameron did not report back. Not then – despite
editorial pressure – when in the year after the Peace
Prize the Doctor's flame burned most bright,
was indeed most vulnerable because the TV cameras
had not yet arrived. Not until after the Doctor died.
It became a meeting with little impact,
far less than Dr Livingstone (Stanley at his side)
opening up Africa to the European scramble,
far less than Mandela and FW de Klerk
who really did change the face of Africa
and shared the Peace Prize for their peace-making.

It was said that Cameron betrayed
his journalistic calling. Maybe he did.
But there was a lot on his mind. The rain-forest,
the river and oppressive heat had him worried.
Resorting to what seems like poetry, he wrote
of the "exuberance of growth full of a sublime
and careless menace". Sublime – menacing – careless.
He formed a similar view of the Doctor in time.
Cameron well knew his history – the theologian who
refocused the study of Jesus, the organist who
refocused understanding of Bach,

the philosopher, humanist, anti-nuclear pacifist
who gave it all up to journey to a forgotten French
colony and found a hospital where
river and jungle overlapped – all of forty years ago,
in the forgotten year before the Great War.

But meeting him, Cameron was nonplussed.
Schweitzer aged 78 was physically a giant –
a self-contained man with a walrus moustache –
who spoke French with an Alsatian accent.
He seemed to be a peasant from another age.
Cameron felt awkward and ill at ease.
Since the Doctor showed little interest in journalism
or him, he turned his attention to three chimpanzees.

Watching one imitating his typing, he thought
of the conundrum of an ape typing Hamlet.
Another he taught to draw and not to eat the paper
or grab at a line and try to eat it.
He noted the squalor of the hospital wards,
where dogs and chickens and children roamed free,
the lack of running water and – except for the theatre
and a gramophone – the total lack of electricity.

Above all he noted Schweitzer's attitude
to the (quotes) *'indigènes'*. There were no African nurses
or doctors, no African sat with them for meals.
Cameron thought this paternalism far worse
than the primitive conditions he'd found.
Schweitzer, he concluded, had scarcely improved
one bit on the foundations he'd laid in 1913.
Twentieth-century progress had left him unmoved.

Cameron had a choice: to go back and
destroy the legend – a truly sensational essay
in iconoclasm - or to leave the old man alone
in his limited, antiquated, devoted way
of serving mankind. So the journalist stayed mute.
Others came and pulled down the temple.
Schweitzer died, Cameron then published
showing how his respect for the Doctor had grown.

Schweitzer's philosophy, scholarship, his music
passed into history. But the hospital remains, Africa
now modernised and cutting edge thanks to
American money. And though the Doctor's claim –
that he and the African were brothers,
with him as the older brother – certainly jarred
with the liberalism of fifty years ago ... and yet
some observers of Africa would find it hard
not to sympathise a little with Schweitzer.
The rush to Democracy is meaningless, he said,
for politics is useless if there is no one
to bore the well hole or bake the bread.

There were angels

None of us believed in angels then
or now but they came all the same
dancing down a sudden beam
to kiss the baby's head, as women
priests do at baptisms -- not that we'd
had her baptised, nor will she him;

a Saturday morning sun, surprising
the circle of sisters, friends who'd come
without ceremony to toast his name
in Earl Grey tea, pink champagne
in wedding present glasses -- and music,
there was music, Mozart most of all.

A similar sunbeam had shone on her
thirty-six years before, such is the gap
now when women must build careers.
Alone in that secular room perhaps
I welcomed the angels and watched
them blessing him, like her years before.

Leipzig Monuments

Proud of its composers, the city repaid its debt
to them in statuary – not as a tourist attraction
but to inspire its children and children's children
and give the older composers resurrection.

* * *

Bach, honoured first in shiny black bronze,
stands before the Thomaskirche – at his back
an array of mighty organ pipes, in his fist
a musical score. This is the Bach

of the preludes, fugues, toccatas and the great
Passacaglia in C minor whose pounding bass
would shake the foundations of a lesser church.
It's Bach with serious learning written on his face –

ignoring the playfulness of the Brandenburgs
and suites written in French or Italian fashion.
Hard to think that he was once neglected until
Mendelssohn resurrected the Matthew Passion.

But Bach knew all about resurrection.
In all of his work there is nothing finer
than that peel of choral joy – *Et resurrexit*
climaxing the Creed of the *Mass in B minor*.

* * *

Mendelssohn's resurrection came courtesy
of 3D imaging, his statue recreated from photos
of the one the Nazis destroyed in 1936.
He stands near Bach but with a romantic pose

in bronze that's as brown as the mottled shadows
in a *Midsummer Night's Dream*. Wagner wrote
that the scherzo was just a tinkling tune
and no Jew could compose music of note.

But didn't that anti-Semite know *Elijah*
and its choruses? Couldn't he applaud the *Octet*,
revise his opinion after the violin concerto?
Did he not thrill to that last intense quartet

Mendelssohn wrote after his sister's death?
He may not have been a revolutionary of tone
but Mendelssohn's was the music of noble feelings
in the tradition of Bach, Haydn, Beethoven.

* * *

Wagner's statue is some distance away - and new,
with bright fresh paint. It shows a small man in a blue
jacket, backed by a large silhouette; his plinth
a cliff edge etched with ghostly figures, who

must be those that Wagner resurrected
from the German unconscious – Wotan, Siegfried,
Brünnhilde and the Valkyries. The Nazis loved Wagner,
but Israel banned him until Barenboim freed

the music from national phobias. So is Leipzig
doing the same, rehabilitating the music of a wayward
son? For this is the city where he was born, his roots
going deeper than either Bach or Mendelssohn.

Wagner's statue epitomizes the dilemma of music
transposed to another medium. Who can follow
an aria when it's set in stone? Was Wagner a genius
or just a small man who cast a huge shadow?

Credo

"In this secular age, the music of JS Bach fills more churches than the worship of J Christ"
                       Ludwig Schlottermann

I believe in Bach, the Father JS,
Maker of heavenly music,
And in his son Johann Christian,
Who was conceived in Leipzig,
Died in London and is buried in St. Pancras
Old Churchyard.

Parodies apart
I cannot be alone in finding in Bach
A warming of the heart and spirit
That is frozen out of organised religion.
Maybe it is because he comes from an age
Before science and secularism, but I find

I can believe in the ghostly power of the Passions,
The spiritual comfort of the cantatas
And the blessings poured forth in the *Mass in B Minor*.
If Newton's God was a mathematician,
Bach emulated him in the *Art of Fugue*,
The intricate patterns of the *Musical Offering*.

I believe in Bach, the Father JS,
Maker of heavenly music,
And in his many sons, not just German
But enthused by his spirit beating out
Rhythms, ricercars, rhapsodies and raps
In every corner of the echoing world.

Memory

She is the soul of politeness. Once
she has focussed on me, she makes a smile
It's good of you to come, How's your wife –
she must have said the same to moustachioed
uncles in the Kaiser's time. We chat a while.

Then: *you know what I'm going to say.*
I say I do: it's the burden of her trance
which no amount of chitchat can relieve.
But say it all the same, I say.
She says: *I no longer want to live,*

sometimes *Ich woll nicht mehr leben.*
It is my cue to try to distract her
to tell her tales of the *Wunderkind*
who told stories from the age of three,
was official classroom raconteur,

youngest contributor ever to the *Tagesblatt*
but wet herself outside the Chancellery
and, this being winter, was forced to walk home
knickerless. She laughs. *You know more
about me than me. You're my memory.*

If only, if I had privileges to wipe her history
clean – not the bits which I repeat but all
she keeps in hidden files to which
access is denied. I can only guess. Guilt that she
could not get her parents out, the fatal fall

of a husband before her eyes, the fact
that despite a life of campaigning she could
not make that difference, that the world
she wants to leave is no better, is so much
worse that the world to which she came.

Camphor

She hadn't noticed the odour before in
hurrying through the dawn along the Rue
La Fayette, until the fourth morning
when it came at her, out of the blue,
caught at her nostrils with the pungent
smell that permeated the house in Calais
– her grandmother's mothballs. It meant
she was sure he would come that day.

He'd insisted on going back to
Berlin – for his family, for friends – and
became caught up in *Kristallnacht*.
He could not telephone or write or send
word of what he would do. Everyone
was in shock. But she willed him to come,
stood all day on the *quai numéro un*
looking north-east, beckoning him.

She knew he could not see her or hear
the pounding of her heart, but sensed that
the scent of her longing, that *odorat d'amour*
they'd shared when their love was secret
would reach him on an autumn breeze,
would hurry him here, as children run
with their dogs when they smell the sea – so
much stronger than camphor or perfume.

Buff

"What's buff?"
Being with a child can put you on your mettle.
Specially when your mouth is full of metal –
screws and pins as you clamber a ladder
to fix a curtain rail for him and his mother,
the rail in one hand, your tools in the other.

"Mmm?"
"What's buff?" Where do you begin with buff?
With that dirty brown colour of leathery stuff
that gave its name to the Royal East Kent's
the regiment of an uncle who died in France?
Steady the Buffs makes no sense.

"I'll come down."
Maybe it's a movie buff the kid has seen
or maybe something a bit more obscene
some celeb, who's appearing in the buff
with others wallowing in their trough
of scandal making an answer tough.

There's the headline –
Terrorists Now Play Blind Man's Buff
and a picture of a hostage, a white kerchief
tied tight across a terror struck face.
But the child has moved to the bookcase
examining coloured photos from space.

So do you address the terror in that typeface
or turn away and accept the breathing space?

Me

Who's that?
It's – me, granddad!
He laughs at the duffer at the other end.
'Me' is four, answers the phone,
rings out when his mother
dials (though of that I'm not sure),
is twenty-five per cent of my genes
but teaches me to play his Gameboy,
can croon along with Crazy Frog,
can't read a newspapers except for
simple headline words like Iraq, War,
Dead – tells me confidently that he will never
be a soldier or handle a gun.

At his age, this me was an evacuee
had left his toys in London – all wood and tin –
but had learned to climb every tree
in the garden, didn't know there were phones
or papers but listened religiously to the wireless,
accumulator-driven, yet was packed off to bed
before the nine o'clock news. All the same
he knew there was a war on, that boys
like him were born to fight Hitler
and wipe the smile off his face,
as the grown-ups said.

At that age, father – fifty per cent of the gene
pool that is me – was packed off to an orphanage,
just as his uncles went over the top at Loos.
Not that Dad knew that though he must have
seen that cigar black Zeppelin flying over.
He never spoke of his childhood, left no diary or letters
except for the copperplate of a seven year old:
Dear Gran, This leaves me well as I hope you are too.
All else is medical records: vaccinated at five,
mumps at seven, rheumatic fever at nine though
still fit enough to sail aged thirty to India
in the second war to end all wars.

Attitude

I've always liked those -tude words –
you know, like longitude or latitude.
I suppose it's because I did Latin.

They're not the sort of words you come
across every day. Just as well perhaps –
try telling your girl you like her pulchritude
and she's probably slap your face. And
never allude to amplitude. Beatitude
used to describe the Sermon on the Mount
or the term of address for the tea-cosy hatted prelate
of a country too small to send us illegal immigrants.
As for claritude, crassitude, crebritude, limpitude
and mollitude – well, I leave you to judge.

But there's one that stands out from the – well,
multitude – partly because it lies at the heart
of the others. I mean where would platitudes or gratitude
be without attitude? It's very much a word for today.
Entire schools of philosophy and behavioural psychology
are devoted to attitude studies. Did you know that attitude
is a function of cognitive, affective, conative components,
according to Maase, Fink and Kaplowitz? Sub-atomic
particles can have attitude – so I'm told.
And actresses, models, sugar-and-spice girls
are said to have attitude if just a glimmer of personality
shines through the glamour. The face under the paint.

Attitude is personal. It's the broken sword and cracked
breastplate with which I've fought the world with
such fortitude and habitude, not to say ineptitude.
That confrontation with the headmaster which shaped
my life: "Why do you behave in that manner?"
"What manner? I've done nothing wrong."
"It's not what you've done, it's your attitude".
He was right. Attitude characterised me, was me.
It could not, cannot, must not be taken away.
I've lived with attitude, I shall die with attitude.
Some people call it the soul.

Berry Head Hotel

Hard to imagine on this benign-sea,
sun-blessing afternoon the gloomy
Reverend Lyte, sitting here complaining
of 'change and decay in all around I see'.

Change, yes – there's a fleet-sized marina
and devil's hordes of body-exposed
tourists between here and his church.
He'd have had to walk with blinkers on.

But decay, no. The vicarage-hotel
is newly painted, lawns mown, geranium
pots dead-headed and watered. Cup Final
crowds who croon 'Abide With Me'

congregate here for continental breakfasts,
camembert baguettes and cream teas.
But, of course, Lyte was writing in winter:
'Swift to its close ebbs out life's little day'.

A Cautionary Tale

i.m. Lotte Moos who gave new meaning to old tales

Jack was a wastrel, he had
no job and spent all day in bed
reading the financial pages
and dreaming of a pad in Dubai.
One day, his mother said:
"Get up, boy, and take the cow
to market. Get a good price
and make sure you bring back the money
so we can buy our food."

Jack went to market and met
a market trader in a coloured
waistcoat who said he would
give Jack five magic beans
for the cow which would make
Jack rich for ever more.
Always trust the market, thought Jack,
and took the beans home.
Now his mother was furious, of course,
scolded Jack and threw
the beans out of the kitchen window.

The next day five strong shoots
had grown, and the day after
there were five trees which entwined
into one gigantic trunk.
Soon people came to look, more
and more, and wanted a stake
in this wondrous growth vehicle.
They bought shares in the Beanstalk
Company, in the Good-Old-Jack Fund,
in Golden Egg Futures and
in the Giant Growth Hedge Fund.
Everybody was happy and Jack
bought his pad in Dubai.

Then there was a drought and

the beanstalk withered and fell.
Some said it was global warming,
others said Jack had cut it down.
There was panic at the market and
people said it was a calamity that should
never have happened. Gradually it emerged
through the media that Jack had already stolen
the goose which laid the golden eggs.

Now, children, you knew he would,
didn't you? So why
didn't you tell the grown-ups?

The Long Grass

'I think we long-grassed it,'
                    Boris Johnson MP

Kicked into the long grass
goes the politician's cliché –
confused as to whether he's talking
about football or cricket,
or an uneven playing field
on which the goal posts keep moving
or even just – a sticky wicket.

The real long grass is a sanctum
for field mice and beetles, where
snakes slither among ox-eye daisies,
where Heath and High Brown Fritillaries
flutter free and rare, where
there's every species of a summer's day
except for the common tired cliché.

Darwin and Mum

1959 – year of Castro and Tibet and Cliff Richard's
debut album – and I was doing homework.
It was a hundred years since the Origin of Species
so Fatty Thomas was teaching us evolution and gave
each of us a picture of the white-beard author.

"Who's that?" said Mum – hovering as she did when she
thought I was writing to a girl. "Charles Darwin," I said.
She tutted and hovered the more. "He's the one who
thought we were descended from apes."

"No, Mum." I put down my fountain pen and turned off
the concert I'd had on as background.
"He merely said that apes and gorillas and men are all
descended from a common ancestor – which makes us
the highest order of mammals, called primates."

"I thought primates were archbishops," she tutted.
"Well, all mammals are warm-blooded and I'm not sure
archbishops are. Incidentally, Linnaeus said that primates
included bats. Perhaps that explains it."

She had to laugh. "No, seriously, young man – that there
Darwin denied that we were made by God and I've always
taught you that God made us in his own image.
That's why he loves us and cares for us, day by day.
He cares for all children, big and small."

"I don't think Darwin denied God, though he did give up
going to church. Religion puzzled and bothered him, but
he did believe that the life we know now evolved from
earlier forms."

"But _you_ believe in God, son, don't you?"
"I don't know, Mum. I think I'm an agnostic, like Darwin."
"I'm terribly disappointed in you, son. You used to be
such a nice, shining-faced choirboy, singing solos up
therein the church. I'm sure your singing brought
         many souls to Jesus."

"Mum, that was a long time ago. I've evolved since then.
Certainly my Adam's apple has."
"But you don't believe in Adam and Eve!"
"It's a story, Mum. It is not supposed to be
scientific fact. Genesis is full of myths."

"You mean untruths." She was getting agitated.
"No, Mum. Myths have a sort of truth, like poetry.
But they are of a different order from science and
the sort of truths Darwin revealed."

She left the room and I could see she was crying.
The next few days were difficult. We did not return
to the subject, but I knew she was upset and hurt.
I made a point of going to church with her that Sunday
and did so periodically, specially after Dad died – not
every Sunday, of course, maybe one in four.

I still do, though it's twenty years since she died.
It's not because I'm any less agnostic – I still believe
the truth of what Darwin wrote, even more so. It's
because she would have wanted me to. And as I get
older ... well, I value more and more
                         the truth embodied in myths.

The Churchyard Yew

For a Daughter Converted to Judaism

Strange tales are told about this tree
how a saintly hermit hollowed out
its heart – or perhaps the carpenter who
    made the pulpit –
how Pontius Pilate as a boy played
in its shade and men with axes punished it –
    perverse in their poverty.
They say it was planted by the church
    but it seems much older.

I stoop under the veil of grounded boughs,
enter a holy gloom and cautiously touch
iron-smooth trunks welded together
    like pillared stone.
Its strength is its age – *a living thing
produced too slowly to decay* but high up
on limbs stained like ancient blood are shoots
    impertinently green.
Spring's conversion makes some trees showy:
    the yew guards its privacy.

Part of me is with you at your Passover
round the old wood table – the meal,
all of you leaning left to drink the wine
    and then the *seder*.
As the youngest it would have been you
who put the questions – in time your child
will ask the meaning and hear how God
    delivered his people.
Part of me, more than just the genes,
    will be with him or her.

I can't say what part – who knows what
made the East End compost where I grew
possibly a Jewish granny but my mother said
    Jesus was her Lord.
Part of me would follow you even though

I fear circumcision and Zion's extremes
part follows my mother's faith and Bach's
    St Matthew Passion.
With clear eyes I look upon the ancient yew
    knowing that Jesus was a Jew.

Lunching by the Sea of Galilee

"Swimming strictly prohibited"
proclaims the board in three languages.
Walking on the water's not mentioned,
but there's something beyond the natural here.
The lunch is heavenly and the waiter
celebrates his tip by discus-hurling
a slab of bread over the broadwalk rail.
"For the fish!" Slim green shivers
gather to bite and fight and –
the bread is gone.

This is peace. A surprising breeze,
swallows swooping low, an avocet
circling ever wider, the Tiberias
rowing club teaching thin, young arms
to pull and feather, and this sea
stretching away to a hazy shore –
and hills which hide the real world
of lookout posts, border guards, weapons of evil.

A certain person came this way,
advising the fishermen,
and slept in their boat,
preaching peace and – as they said –
casting his bread upon the waters.
But there were sharks here then, quick
to seize anyone rising to take the bait –
guardian sharks ensuring two thousand
years without peace,
constantly breeding, constantly evolving.
They are still here, somewhere,
hidden in the haze.

Roadside Stop

In America they'd call it a diner
no one here would dine in such
a place with white tie and wine.
It's more of a snacker, a shack
beside an abandoned filling station
"exit only through the forecourt"
on the inland fringe of a county famous
here to be seated" – please wait while the
waitress with the pierced eyebrow chats
up a youth in leather, while you read the front
of the free tabloid you'd never be seen dead reading
at home, while a cat outstares you at the window,
while you try to work out which couple came
in the anti-rust painted Renault, while dust
motes dance in a sudden sunbeam, while a plump
woman appears from the kitchen wiping hands
on her apron and smiles a guileless smile,
says "Sorry to keep you waiting" in an accent
rich in rusticity – and you know
this is the heart of England.

Scrap-Iron words

They come out of the blue, unbidden
words, furtive phrases insinuating themselves
dropping on my thoughts like verbal junk-mail.
As I walk out the door, I hear rebalancing
and am told 'spik Inglish'. Not speak – 'spik'
but why? Later it's twelfth-century – nimby –
backlash – gringo. Not all at once.
Spaced out so they're unexpected.

I know full well it's regurgitation –
undigested words from yesterday's radio or
reading. Or maybe not undigested but
selected by the Unconscious Committee
on Neologisms, chosen to be clichés of the month.
All the same I'm puzzled to learn
29 of the singers are black. And cantus firmus
which I know but have to look up. Then
Herman Van Rompuy – yes, I know who he is but
I don't wish to meet him now, thank you.

I guess it's a symptom of ageing, that my mind
no longer controls its own vocabulary. Or maybe
a new form of random thought – suitable for poetry.
But what poems could come from stringing
together unrelated words, unless it be the literary
equivalent of scrap-iron sculptures – bits
welded together but you wonder how they stay up:

spindly – Leveson – looming – gutsy – networking –
clawed back – Sir Christopher Mayer – biggest yet –
gringo – tweeting – Red Nose Day – fridge-door –
password – courageous dad – electronically – finally –
potholes – potholes – potholes.

Foldings

The geometry of my duvet defeats me.
The sodden lump I carry from machine
to line laughingly offers a corner,
dares me to grasp it, which week by week I do
to find not two surfaces flapping but four
tucked into six or ten teasingly
inside out. Somewhere there's a manual:
HOW TO HANG OUT YOUR DUVET –
doubtless in Swedish, untranslated.

Simpler were the sheets mother brought
by pram in the bagwash, which we'd fold
and hang in the drying shed, and fold again,
when hot and soap scented, for the basket home –
four hands for four corners treading the boards –
meet your partners, take the sheet,
don't drop it, lad, just keep it neat.
If I'd been taller she younger we could have kissed
above the folds.
                    In that lost world
everything existed in folds – letters
in tiny envelopes, linen, handkerchiefs
(initials uppermost), trousers with creases,
paper darts, aeroplanes, aerograms,
consequences and birds with beaks that gawped
as you pushed and pulled – a world before it was
decreed that all news must unfold, all dramas,
events, situations, relationships must hang out,
be free, straightened out, demystified
for everyone to see.
                    I met a scientist
who said after the genome the new frontier
was protein folding. This was a new world
of alpha-helixes and alpha-hairpins,
of globules and polypeptide chains that in
in a millionth of a second spontaneously fold
themselves into intricate three-dimensional shapes.
But why? *That's what we are trying to find out,*
he said: *proteins are the action triggers of life.*

A protein's function depends on the way it's folded.
If we can find out why it folds so and how
then we may be able to cure genetically based diseases.

So not all matter is straight and open to view.
Not at all. So life is rather like my duvet
which spontaneously folds itself into intricate
three-dimensional shapes. *Life is very much*
like your duvet. Which is comforting as I struggle
to prevent it falling into the flower bed.

The Secret

For Patricia Oxley

We swam together once,
two shivering figures at Fishcombe
without even a seal as chaperone –
more accident than assignation.
William lay ailing at the Mount.
What struck me were her quick
strokes as she crossed the cove,
the clothes arranged neatly on the rocks,
her good sense – 'the secret is
not to get your hair wet', she said
as if to a daughter or her grandsons.
And her modesty, of course.

We adore her cooking, admire
her kitchen's order, her garden's colour,
amaze at the quality you can count on
in her poetry journal, know that
her festivals will function more efficiently
than the trains that take us there.
Her excellence is of no modest order.
The secret is not to get your hair wet.

In the Present

It was a true magic that neither of them
could have made to happen –
an impromptu stop, getting going again
delayed by the cavalcade behind a traction
engine creeping up the hill, the wander to kill
time into a churchyard where the fierce sun
rebounded from Cotswold stone and was quenched
in the lime trees' shadow.

They sat on a bank, began to talk
but she pushed him back, laid her head
on his chest. He tried to rise and
look into her eyes, to kiss or to question
but she plaited his legs with hers
and he lay back with her
living in the present

   – like the swifts
soaring far above, forgetful of past journeys,
neglectful of dangers to come.

February

An early spring, a warm sun
blackbirds play tag one by one.
In the shade snowdrops cascade
down a bank under tall trees.
You hear a first skylark's song
and I see it now on the wing
glinting against the sun.
It's time for smiles from friend
to friend and I'm glad of all
the efforts you have made
to keep love warm till spring stayed.

Down a Grassy Track

Until the bend is reached, about half-way down,
With tight-leafed May the narrow path is lined
And arching strands of still bare briars.
On evenings like this for those from town
It's a tempting walk, if they have in mind
To savour shadows and the rooks' raucous choirs.
But, all the same, townsmen should be warned
It's a short-cut to nowhere, nor does it lead
To moated manor house, field or barn.
All the walker can do is turn and retrace
His steps.   So it is with my words which lead
Nowhere, neither wooing nor flattering her face
For the first has been long since neglected
And the other, though much to my taste,
Would now be quite roundly rejected.
So my words go nowhere but down a grassy track,
Hidden in shadow, and then to the road turn back.

My Easter rising

The blossom may be mimicked in snow
and there's no telling what this spring
will bring before March marches off.
But I'm done with all that winter stuff.
The gloom has melted all away
for you are my classic spring day,
my promise of sun after showers,
my rainbow, my darkness quickly shedding the hours,
my Easter rising (no, not the Dublin sort),
my rediscovery of the long-lost art
of laughing with the sun and singing
with all the new season is bringing,
my exultation at the changing skies above,
my jubilation, my joy, my longing, my love.

Uncollected Poems

Passing into Light

i.m. Susan Homans Elias

Here it's a muted long shadow morning
the river the deep green of deepest sleep.
The sun raises itself on one elbow.
Cygnets pass like grey clouds among the white.
Where you were until a week ago there
is still darkness but you now live in light
perpetual, as our belief affirms,
floodlighting the lives of you and yours
even back to the Adams presidents
and forward to grandchildren yet to come.

Beyond a school fence trees form a low vault
and sycamore seeds spin like propellers
from a single taut spider's thread, glinting
as they spin, like a cut glass chandelier.
In Greece they install chandeliers even
in the smallest chapels on the highest rocks,
their power cables looped over pines
many metres below and all so that
lights may shine once a year upon the few
who ascend to celebrate the saint's day.
Shrines on the peaks always commemorate
Elijah or as they say *Profitis*
Elias. I think of what you can now see,
Susan, from your sunlit mountain peaks.

In the Garden of the Villa Cimbrone

You lay half in sun, half in shade
translating Montale, but the unexpected
April heat drove me under the clipped yews
studying their neat contours – smoother
than the unclipped rock-sprouting hills.

We had been here the night before, alone
in the dusk, and at the turn of the path debated
whether to return would spoil the memory. But broad
daylight brought statues into bright relief,
sharpened shadows, revealed intriguing inscriptions.

Did DH Lawrence really pen the verse on the wall
where Mercury crouches? Did Greta Garbo and
Leopold Stokowski share much more than
an *Ore di Segreta Felicitá* when they came here
to escape the *Clamore di Hollywood*?

This legendary ledge above Amalfi brims with questions,
contrasts. We sit on a sun-baked balcony – you
with Camomile tea and cakes, me with Campari soda
and green globe olives. An indecisive ant
rushes from the red to the green and back again.

Holiday Rain

We thought nothing of it at first:
the earth was hard, grass scorched,
we needed it we said, searching the sky
for the crease of a smile to see
when it would pass. Then we stopped
glancing up, and looked within for
diversions in books, cards and chat,
shutting out the world of droop and drip.
We roused with products of the oilman's art –
anoraks, spongy trainers against the wet,
umbrellas as gaudily big as any estate
agent could wish – and travelled
in steamed-up buses to queue behind
other anoraks for tea in plastic cups.
Still we looked down, willing
puddles be still and mirror our hopes.
It rained for days until all oils
and phenols were purged. In the smiles
of the warming west we looked up again
into a shower of holiday rain.

Warnings of Severe Weather

There are floods in the west on the Severn
and Wye – warnings of severe weather:
on telly Ian McAskill, who famously missed
the hurricane, says no one can forecast extremes,
only the bits in between. Yet suddenly
there's enough blue for a battleship's crew.
An angler sun casts thin shadows
as long as the black rods across the river.

Tired from motorway miles driving in spray
I glance at the blue, immediately know
my mistake. A spot leaps at my eyes,
sits there, expands like the orange cones
flashes its warning – wire black

against the fridge door, white against shadow –
an arrow generated on some neuron screen
e-mailing age, a headache to come.

Beastly Weather

Just weeks and the beast-from-the-east
was devastating growth and green.
We stared at blackened stems,
bare sticks, our nurturing of nature
aborted in a late Spring.

But May mocks our mistake.
We walk on Widbury Hill and sit
on a mound (avoiding the thistles)
amid a profusion neither I nor any
garden catalogue can ever name –

pinks blooming straight out of stones,
white petals smaller than a child's
finger nail, secretive yellows, blues
that would make a forget-me-not blush –
all within a hand's breadth.

We are obsessed with weather,
watch it web-wise whenever we can.
But weather happens. The beast
was just another troublesome creature
from the east. Like ancient bears and wolves

it came and it went. The flowers
on Widbury took no notice.

The Fishmonger

Willowy, bleached like a bone,
in loose netted suit,
his eyes questioning shoppers
left and right: do you recognise me?
do you know what's happened?
Knowing or not knowing,
they still picture him
in stretched apron stripes,
robust, rotund, surrounded by
his men gutting and cutletting,
too busy to eye the customers
as the fish heads do.
The best fresh fishmonger for
miles around, patron of
an ancient natural trade.

His darting eyes evoke
other, endless questions.
Will the service of his shop
survive, will the slab still
teem with shells, ice, fish
or being empty grow green,
will our families have to be fed
on fillets and fingers frozen
on supermarket shelves?

Our past walks away
with that willowy man
in the loose netted suit.

The shoals are leaving our shores.

Lazarus

Mornings he shuffles
from the estate down into town
and back, never stopping,
never looking right or left
though his eyes do spy passers-by.
One hand clutches an oil-soiled coat
tight about his body like a shroud,
the other a holdall. He goes to the supermarket,
buys a plastic-wrapped sandwich and
carton – it's his routine, his liturgy.
He's not clean shaven – not clean
anything – but doesn't have a beard.
The bristles on his face match those on top.
Kids call him gooseberry or hedgehog:
    Squash him flat, squash him flat,
    just like a hedgehog.
    Hear him go splat.

Adults call him Laserhead – to do with his name
He was in the paper, a sort of miracle
but that was long ago. The local rag
asked him what it had felt like: he said
he'd felt nothing or couldn't remember
so they asked his sisters instead. But
it was a long time ago and one sister's dead,
the other's in a home and no one
remembers now. The sisters left
him the house but not enough money
for electricity. You don't need electrics
on the other side, they say.
Laserhead shuffles back from town
muttering: 'mustn't look back', 'mustn't look back'.
Is he afraid of being followed or is he
just passing the time between sandwiches,
waiting for a miracle?
– Another miracle?

George

On the carrier of his bike
is strapped one of those white wooden boxes
you don't see now, made for kippers
or something – they made excellent
fire wood. Canvas shopping
bags hang from the handles. He pedals
slowly, weaving and tacking like a sailor.
He used to try not to until he read that a corrupt
politician had promised to go straight – after
which George no longer bothered. His wife
said he acquired his sense of humour late in life.
About the same time he knocked over a motorbike
and its rider accused him of pedalling like a tank.
Funny really. George wears a baggy blazer,
trousers clipped at the ankles and a Trilby.
He's small, smiling, red-faced – friendly
but people don't talk to him, except on Remembrance Day
– the actual Remembrance Day,
the Eleventh, not the Sunday thing.
Then he wears a beret with a battered
tank badge and his medals.
There's a couple of stars, the orange and green
Defence Medal and another red, navy
with three white stripes. That's the MM.
He was in the desert, a sergeant. Talk to him
and he'll tell you it was for dragging
his officer out of the turret and going
back to rescue the rest of the crew.
"The captain told me to. I was
a soldier under authority, carrying out
orders. So they needn't have given
me a medal but they did.
At least it made me Mum
and me intended proud."

Treasury

I called it the Treasury but only
to myself. What I said out loud,
when I thought I'd found favour
by clearing my plate, was
Can I play the piano?

I couldn't play, I was no Mozart
at seven, and the answer after
a long stare and a clucking of
her tooth was – *You may*,
but don't you touch anything.

'Anything' was everything crowded
into that cold, uncarpeted room,
the things I could see over my shoulder
as I crashed chords, poked out tunes --
silver cruets, cut glass, candlesticks
green like celery, studio photographs,
browning prints in old gilt frames.

By pounding God Save the King
with my left hand I could just about
reach the lacquered trinket box
beside a cake stand but never
the drawer stuffed with letters, though
I stretched and hoped. If I stopped
playing she would come in at once.

These were her treasures from a
bombed out flat by the docks,
the wealth of a woman who'd managed
a chocolate factory, hired out
hand-me-downs to the unemployed,
whose unusual enterprise had been
blighted by the Blitz.

She died years ago after a
bitter, mostly silent old age and I
never learned to play the piano.

Into East Anglia

It's a good straight road for cars,
camper-vans and caravans; not many
juggernauts until you join the A14 for
Felixstowe. Good for a bit of motoring,
as they used to say, even to glimpse
the panels of the Solar Park flashing through
the hedgerows. As I pass, my hand grips
the wheel tighter with the memory
of family bliss crumbling. Not the empty
back seat as now, but children suitcases –
sweat and noise. 'Can we stop?
I need to go.' 'Can't you wait?' 'No'.
So somewhere near Babraham or was it
Wilbraham? I found a side-road and backed
into a concealed cart-track, switched off
the engine and off they went three daughters,
plus their mother glad to get away
from the driver whose driving she deplored.
Back on the A14, five miles on, a scream
came from the back seat: 'I've left it behind!'
It was a hat covered in badges and tokens.
'All right, we'll go back.' 'No, we won't.'
But the car had already stopped and was turning
into another lane in search of a by-road
which would take us back to Wilbraham
(or was it Babraham?) and the lost hat.
Eventually we found the road with the first
cart-track and the treasured hat.

It was a time before global warming and solar
panels, before I owned a decent car for motoring,
a time when a family was growing up around me
and I took sparse notice of them or the emerging
anger of their mother – a time when we had just
joined the 'Common Market' as they called it,
when politics meant hope and when I thought
I'd be a writer.

Wiping Their Faces

I've come to wipe their faces
with my bucket, cloths and kitchen
scourer to scrub away the grey-green
patches, careful not to raise the lead
which spells out Missed by All and
Their New Life Together. Not that
I could or would have wiped their
faces until they lay here together.

He died in her arms, breathing faintly –
just perceptibly – as the tumour
pressed against his heart (I'd done
a circuit of suburban pharmacies the week
before to get a drug to quicken his pulse.)
Then she said he seemed to sigh and that
was that. Afterwards she washed his face,
laid him out and telephoned.

She died in a distant ward – a week
after she crossed the road looking back
at a passing car into the path of the one
behind. The broken thigh sent an embolism
slowly toward her heart. She should have had
physiotherapy but probably they thought her
too old. But at least one of the nurses washed
her face, telephoned and told me
not to hurry.

So I go from time to time to wash their faces
as they lie together, snugly, one on top of the
other – in their new life together which will last
as long as civilisation lets this cemetery last.

The Rare Plant of Runnymede

The lawns are cut, the monuments scrubbed,
but make no mistake, this was once a noxious
swamp like the treaty John signed (under duress, he said)
to ward off rebellion and raise taxes.

The Latin was crammed with fish weirs, old wine,
sureties, evil customs about forest laws,
the legal limits imposed on women,
when the barons could take to the battlefield,
and how to avoid debts due to Jews –
all reeking of their time, all now repealed.

Yet one sweet-smelling clause survives – like the rare
water dropwort (*oenanthe aquatica*) in a nearby field –
that no free man shall be seized or imprisoned,
stripped of his rights, outlawed or exiled,
… except by the lawful judgement of his equals
or by the law of the land. The dropwort or water
parsley is a medicinal plant with a scent
like wine; some forms are thought poisonous.

Elevated into law in England and its erstwhile colonies,
that great clause is universally recognised
as an affirmation of the values of democracy,
human rights and the Rule of Law, a foundation
of the freedom of the individual against despots,
a cornerstone of the American Constitution.
They came together to celebrate the octocentenary
of Magna Carta on 6.15.15 (by US reckoning).

On 7.4.15 writers, directors, members of the parliament
almost as old as the Great Charter petitioned the US
for the release of Shakar Aamer, the last British resident
at Guantanamo Bay – imprisoned without charge
or trial for thirteen years. The irony – or history's
lesson, if you will – is that two US presidents cleared
Aamer for release years before. He remains imprisoned
because the barons of the Pentagon regard Magna
Carta as a mouldy manuscript, a poisonous weed.

John Lilburne Waiting

"John Lilburne came this day to Ware; but things not succeeding at the Rendezvous came not further."
   William Clarke, secretary of the Army Council, to the Speaker of the House of Commons, November 1647.

Spurred on by God and his creed
of Englishmen born free,
he rode twenty miles through the mud
to wait in an inn through the day.

The cold pewter made him start –
ale soaking the proud moustache
which in the Archbishop's court
had shaken with righteous rage.

Now he sat silent and still,
watching and wondering how
things went on a nearby hill
at the army's Ware rendezvous.

Papers were stuck in men's hats
with *England's Freedom* writ bold
and demands for *Soldiers' Rights*
the officer class to behold.

Fairfax, the general (though fair)
with Cromwell – a friend of Lords
and an armour-plated squire –
they too would read his words.

He was sure the people were winning
as he won in his finest hour
against muskets, gags and whipping
and a nightly cell in the Tower.

Small boys came in to stare
at his tasselled breeches and boots;
he showed a Leveller could wear
what the grandees wore by rights.

A messenger came at last:
Cromwell had triumphed through blood,
one man lay dead, the day lost;
his mottoes trodden in the mud.

He rode off by the setting sun
to wait in his cell on Tower Hill
for England's freedom to be won.
– Some say he is waiting still.

The Skylark

It might as well have had no body
like Shelley's blithe spirit, for as
a child I never saw or heard a skylark.
They did not chirrup above the London traffic
or hover over our soot-sewn park.

I first heard one on a firing range
where we aimed at distant plywood men
with unwieldy bren or stuttering sten
and there it was in the lull – of guns and
sergeant's shouts – a trill as high as cirrus.

Vaughan Williams too was thinking of guns
as he watched soldiers leave for France
and sketched as the theme of The Lark
Ascending, the spirit of its agitated call
without the endless repetition – of bird or guns.

Now it's only you that hears one:
"There's a lark up there somewhere."
I strain eyes along your extended arm –
in vain. But bless you, VW, for the compensation
of your music for the bird to me silent.

And Blackbirds shall inherit the Earth

There had to be a use for the neighbour's
silver birch – its silver days long past
now that ivy hobbles the trunk and the upper
limbs are skeletal grey.

Pigeons come and go, but every evening
a blackbird, its back to the setting sun,
engages in debate with a rival
in a garden somewhere near.

Its recitative is elaborately simple –
two bars of a liquid melody

the arpeggios signed off with stitches
from a high piccolo.

It's a code of course – not random
but as meaningful as any Bach
fugue, telling the rival that whatever
humans may do to their world

there will always be the evening sun
and bare branches and worms
and delicious decay ... and that blackbirds
will inherit the earth.

A Not-so-Green Bird

The only bird we had was a budgerigar
– it was my sister's – we used to let it out
to fly around the flat
until Gran, in flapping all-day slippers,
trod on it. I was reminded of budgie
by the bird I saw on the black seed feeder,
usually monopolised by gaudy goldfinches
until bullied aside by greenfinch greed.

It was a linnet – long-tailed, with white-
edged wings, its breast pink and proud.
All I knew about linnets was the song
Gran taught us in her toothless way:

*My old man said follow the van
and don't dilly-dally on the way.
So off went the van with our home packed in it
and I walked behind with me old cock linnet.*

Now linnets are rare – or supposed to be –
and they are finches. In fact, Wordsworth
thought a greenfinch was a green linnet
and rhapsodised about it in romantic
fashion. At Grasmere now, the English Lakes
scent factory is selling Green Linnet Perfume

– 24.95 for a screw top bottle,
12.95 for the spray.

But the true linnet is making a come-back.
A scientist with the RSPB discovered
they were saved by feeding on oil seed rape,
that yellow stain upon the landscape.
So the linnet is not so green after all.
For me the little fella spelled freedom –
freedom from the fierce winds of February,
freedom from for ever thinking about the economy,
freedom from being a caged up singer,
and then at the mercy of any Granny
tramping about in flip-flop slippers.

Heron

It sails on large wings over the willows
languid like an Empire flying boat,
its neck tucked in – characteristically –
yet it's buzzed by a pair of rooks who
see it as an attacking bird of prey
which – given the opportunity – it would be.

I saw it earlier pretending to be a cardboard
cut-out – a sliver of a stick beside the water.
It's a creature of contradictions, greedy yet
a paragon of patience, diffident as a wader,
alone among water fowl not swimming
(though it can), a flyer that never wishes to hurry.

I'm struck by its beauty, its elegance, singularity
but others see it differently. Because it's said
to defecate when disturbed, Americans call it
a 'shitepoke' which is also an insult
for a thin weakly person – thin, yes, but weakly?
Ask any fish for an opinion about that!

Founders' Day

It could be genetically encoded this
assignation of cygnets, only the swans
can tell and they are mute.
They've been gathering for weeks, three
resident pairs, then twenty, forty-one –
the last count: sixty-eight
stretched silk necks against the dark
town shore.
                In nineteen forty, a young
evacuee's box camera caught
them flocking by the bridge; eighteen
ninety and a maltster's wife did them
in watercolours, their bright
plumes now faded with her paper;
fifty years before in a passing curate's
diary just a brief note;
then nothing until year one of William
and Mary and a Quaker's admonition
(dressed plainly for the part):
"We have no need of warbling for behold
the swans that multiply along our river
in silence please their Lord."

Earlier in Elizabeth's reign
a pair of swans was etched on the head
of the fabled Great Bed, and a poet
named Vallans claimed that Venus,
her very self, sent wingèd Mercury
to Italy to steal a cygnet pair;
and when he brought them
to the River Lea Jove blessed them.
Their offspring, said Vallans, replenished
the Severn, Humber and the Trent
"yea, even the verrie Thames."
It was this royal pair, ancestors of all
England's swan horde that
decreed a congress every fifty years
or so between Ware Priory and the bridge
the very flock we look at now.

They crowd the bank preening – their smooth
necks mellowing from milk to cream as they
twist this way and that
with ever active beaks. The legend lasts
until the cook at a riverside pub is seen
scattering yesterday's bread
upon the water and swans with geese
and ducks in unusual numbers all
fight for human's food.

Five fingers

For six days I shared my morning shave
with a whisp of a creature so thin and white
I could scarce discern it, search as I might
on the walls and ceiling and plaster cove.
The odd creeping spider I'd welcomed oft
but this was a fellow seen first in flight,
a blur of wings before folding tight
umbrella like, a white plume moth.
Five fingers its Linnaean name,
Aciptilia pentadactyla to be precise,
a nocturnal flyer found in shrubs and grass
but seldom in bath or other bright room.
The seventh day it left without fuss or apology,
my silent lesson in Lepidopterology.

Jackson's Wood

It could have been a slip of the cartographer's
pen, a bubble in a line
out beyond the new estates,
slowly being sliced away,
plough-planed,
by a businessman farmer
obsessed with squared-off fields.

We stopped him our group when
someone told the council
of the April carpet of wood anemones,
testimony all agreed to a remnant
of ancient woodland irreplaceable,
for centuries free from the plough.

Jackson's wood they named it
(ironically after that farmer)
and kids on mountain bikes
became licensed to race
down ribbons of black mud
between arches of fluted trees –
bluebells all gone but anemones untouched.

The trees though tell a truer story –
slender trunks twisting up from coppiced parents
unnoticed in the level mud – hornbeam,
the timber few tools can fashion,
grown here as fuel for an industry
once important, now forgotten.

Brown malt was kilned nearby over
hornbeam fires – slow-burning giving flavour
to malt for porter ale for men
whose portering twisted and strained
young limbs recently risen from
coppiced country parents.

Hornbeam now brushed aside by
straight young limbs on mountain bikes.

Post Wood

i.m. Michael Ottley

Men change, we know, for good or ill
but woods change as well.   This
is called ancient woodland, but ancient
it ain't. There's hornbeam planted
among the oaks for furnace fuel,
laurels as cover for pheasants
and an avenue of sweet chestnuts to please
some la-di-dah lady of the house.

So all the ladies of all the houses
came gathering nuts in May
trampling down bluebells as if
it was the opening of the summer sales.
You showed them the red card with
brushwood piles and keep-off signs
tacked to tree trunks.
The ladies cried foul and had you banned.
It was something like moving the goalposts
and certainly no level playing field.

The real miracle is how you changed,
from a Monday to Friday metal basher
with much boozing after the match
Saturdays – to would-be woodman, planting
out oaks you'd raised from acorns,
recording where the nightjar nested,
dedicating dead trees for future wildlife,
guarding the coveys where the muntjac
deer shelter. Shy like you, shunning the
chatter and laughter of local ladies.
Woods change for good or ill
but so do men as well.

The Meads

It serves the planners' purpose – this patch of wetland
prevents two towns from joining arms and armchairs.
Too damp to build on, but anything can be drained now.
A bit of green belt keeps the bandits at bay –
especially if the dampness gets damper day by day.

The wildlife people's purpose is to keep the grass short,
grazed by black Angus pedigrees (oligarch toys), so that
saxifrage, marsh dock, rare lesser sea spurrey,
and 250 species of wildflower can flourish.
They've all been recorded.   Take our word for it –
                    we won't tell you where.

The cattle do their bit. Volunteers keep the ditches clear,
for wintering stonechats. Seven breeds of warbler.
Summer sees dragonflies. Pipistrelles and Natterer bats
spend evenings gorging on insects.
                    Otters have been seen.

If only the speeding commuters and those in half-hourly
trains would look, take notice, approve
even visit but respectfully in twos and threes –
no push chairs please, perambulators, motorcycles:
there's a paved path for pedal cycles beside the river.

Despite the wildlife trust, there are wildernesses.
Shoulder-high thistles, cow parsley, rosebay willow herb,
soldiers-and-sailors, though in white – 'lady spilt the milk'
– stand in clumps as if some medieval open-field farmer
was stocking his (or probably her) herbal larder.

These acres have a history. A criss-cross of drains,
channels, paths, rails, a viaduct have scored the earth –
most now hidden unless you know where to look.
Nature and time chamfered the lines,
closed up the wounds of gashes no longer valid.

A Roman road is a bulrush mound, Robert
Mylne's Marble Gauge is pitted and weathered

like a Georgian tombstone, the four-foot drain's
buried in a dog-rose embankment that separates
a lagoon of gulls from reservoirs reserved for ducks.

The wounds cut deep into history here.
The legions dragged slaves down Ermine Street:
the shackle's in the museum, carefully cleaned of DNA.
Earl Gilbert paid for his disobedience, dragged
from the stirrups, his body bumping across the Meads.

Dick Arnold fared no better, musket-balled on Cromwell's
orders for standing up for democracy and soldiers' rights.
Who knows how many navvies died digging the New
River or laying the railway tracks? They're careful to stop
the carnage now – Samaritans' signs at all crossings.

Tread purposefully over the Meads: look for the saxifrage
if you must. But smell the grass, ruffle the reeds,
avoid the nettles, keep your dog from frightening
the coots. Feel the sun, the wind in your face
and think of the thousands who tramped here before.

Notes: the Meads between Ware and Hertford were crossed by Roman Ermine Street. Nearby is Chadwell Spring, the original source of London's New River and the 1770 Marble Gauge that measured water the New River Company took out of the River Lea.
In 1241, Gilbert Marshall, Fourth Earl of Pembroke, held a tournament here against the orders of King Henry III and in 1647, at the 'Ware Mutiny', three Levellers were court-marshalled by Cromwell and drew lots to see who would be executed by the other two: Trooper Richard Arnold lost and was shot.

Amwell Magna

But for the bridge, you'd not
notice the old river
marked off from the great-lake
gravel pits by ridges of scrub
like a faint slip-stream glimpsed
in a cumulus sky.

Hikers, birdwatchers bent
low by their lenses,
cross with scarcely a glance for
it does not teem with wildlife –
just two lazy mallards
avoiding the crowds.

But look into its flow and
there is a highway
of elvers and lampreys
and the patient pike that
Isaak Walton named
the "freshwater wolf."

I perch for hours above
the old river peering
into the bridge's shadow for
meaning in water which
carries strangers and danger
without the say-so of locks.

Churston

Not the village, nor the ancient inn,
but the inlet, cliff-enclosing Churston Cove
that mugs the memory – a calm sea
for seals and cormorants within a crescent
of woodland and the stony hog's back
rising through hewn rock and boarded
steps to a sort of heaven. Hundreds
of feet below a dog barks –
eat your heart out Albert Hall for that acoustic.

We came here first in the grey days
of John Major – the golf course fence
had nine holes which admitted a curious dog:
now nine hundred holes. Nearby
Agatha Christie once stayed, writing
'Murder on the Links' while lackeys
for the Churstons, Lord and Lady,
served her tea or something stronger.

The St. Pancras Way of Death

a homage to Thomas Hardy

1.

It's not famous like Père Lachaise
or crowded like Bunhill Fields – just
a garden shaded by London planes, known
to dogwalkers and Eurostarters with time to kill.
Old Tom would have loved our springer
which heads for a spot where food's been left.
"Are you digging on my grave?" a lonely
cadaver asked. Yes, replied her little dog,
but only because I hid a bone here.

The dead always want to tell their stories,
not all to be taken seriously – like those
disturbed at levelled Wimborne Minster
"and mixed like human jam". At least here
their slabs don't pave a pissing place.
Sorry, Tom, but that's what you wrote at first.
It was your boss Blomfield who laughed most
when a coffin burst and two skulls fell out.
But you compensated with the Hardy Tree –

packing the headstones around an ash –
the punch-cards of the dead. It was
your earliest architectural design, though
it did not win a medal – a serrated plinth
more serene than common egg-and-dart
launching a living column to the heavens.
The ash completed your work of art,
hugging the stones to herself,
covering them in a blanket of bark.

2.

The forty-foot pit was not your design
for the thousands the railway threw up –
"where we are huddled none can trace".

It was saintly Angela who rescued some names
'of interest' her dial recording Catholics and courtiers,
a marquis or two, a marshal of France, musicians
aplenty – Pasqualino, Mazzinghi, Bach J.C. –
a famous spy, the Chevalier d'Eon, a Turkish
ambassador, an actress who became a lady.

"The dead will rise, retake the life God gave.
Creation's Saviour bless Earth's opening grave".
Never, not ever did she or Tom conceive
that another railway would open the graves –
for another station of longer Eurostar
platforms with yet another station tunneling
in the Thameslink earth beneath. Hardy's
men worked before the trains arrived; here
the busy rails kept rattling – beneath, beside.

3.

The Hardys, Blomfields, the Burdett-Coutts
of the twenty-first century did not make
jokes, erect monuments. They were not poets
but archaeologists, osteologists, scientists
all, interested not just in names but with
the diseases of Dickensian London, the ages,
relationships – the many stories bones can tell.
The dead are always there, often in the way,
but they can be eloquent – provided we listen.

Kingsway

It was built for proconsuls to process
past imperial turrets and classic steeples
to confer with the leaders of younger nations
(Over whom, of course, King George held sway)
in marble halls, themselves addressing
the 'friendship of English-speaking people'.

The imperialists' vulgar tongued relations
like those from Holloway and Newington Green
were confined beneath the new boulevard,
buried in trams which eventually disgorged
their shaken contents beside the Thames.
The poor, though with us, are best not seen.

Now the triumphs and trams have had their day.
From the tunnels the people have long emerged
and stride to work with resolute aims
in groups of twos and threes or singly,
marching like ants, buzzing like flies
past spiders' webs spun for their pay
by nine building societies including
the Northern Rock and Bradford and Bingley.
Empire building is back in another guise.

Nine down and outs sat by the gutter,
waiting for bread from the Methodist Hall.
In a nearby window a young sign writer
was painting in gold upon the plate glass
like a careful housewife spreading butter.
The dossers began to laugh and call
and the painter's grip on his brush grew tighter.
They embarrassed the young man, his gold
line was shaking, but this just encouraged
the tramps to jeer more. At last he retired
and came out again with a tarpaulin screen
to hide from their scorn. Though the nine old
men had now entered the building to forage
for charity, the privacy of the screen endured.
The regilding of Kingsway goes on unseen.

Winter Journey

Rails snake over the snow to some
distant point in op-art strokes so narrow,
neglected ledges are now bright diagonals
framing buildings, fixing whole
backdrops of dull brick in relief.
Dumps, coal heaps are hidden and
all the long, industry-stained line,
that oil-black to London track,
lies sheathed in virgin white.

Here images glimpsed are immediate,
impressions snatched and sketched.
Beside the tracks, traces of ochre
stroked by some Japanese sable
imply grasses newly planted
and a factory is a pendant between
two washes of different white,
a pearl set on an imperial breast,
a majestic mound of Muscovite domes.

But in this aquatinted emptiness
it was not sky flakes that fell to
drape and bury an unbeautiful world.
They are not snow drifts there settled
in sharp elbows round the chimneys,
making shadows on the sheer white roofs.
No snow fell. It was the pure paper
that surfaced and sucked clean
the multi-chrome mess daubed by men.

Sense is transformed in the suburbs,
but in the city the very surface
of the paper is so pocked and pitted
that no whiteness can ever emerge.
Snow here is churned like ash in the sugar,
like windscreen glass it litters the walk,
staining the near and distant streets.
Here the permanent deep world of the grey
neither snow, time nor imagination changes.

Nancy's Funeral

i.m. Nancy Hope (1929-2016)

There was a New Zealand connection, though
it was shelved for that day. The funeral
was a farming affair in a village
that wasn't really a village
in a church that was more like a barn
or a Victorian dolls' house made
of neat brown bricks, perched
on the corner of a busy road that
fed a feeder route to the M6 –
specially busy as that day
the motorway was stationary from
Junction 16 to Junction 20.
Brick lorries, tractors made the church tremble.

She had lived in the village all her life,
helped harvest the wartime corn,
bussed her way to school and work
then nursed a slowly sinking parent
before inheriting the house, letting
lanky nephews camp in the garden,
cycling to church perched on the saddle
before a fall and despite the flatness
of the fields, and her life, going downhill
but not before she had planned
her funeral – the hymns, the readings,
what the vicar should say and should not say.

We perched in the Sunday School gallery,
the ledge for hymn books just above
knee height, resisting the temptation
to rain papers on the bald pates below
or hover like a Stanley Spencer angel
above the sea of grey. The gallery
was a Health and Safety nightmare –
bodies in black squeezed on narrow
benches, knees touching. It took
the best part of an hour for us

to descend the steep stair, our patience
buoyed up by hopes of the wake, planned
by Nancy in the hall next door.

But not before she had been
laid to rest, lowered into a canvas
lined slit in the damp earth
between ranks of family and friends,
earth and roses rained upon her.
It was then that the sodden turf
trembled, perhaps through the passing
of a brick lorry, or the presage of trains
on the HS2 line the farmers fear,
or maybe Nancy chuckling to find
so many friends squeezed into the church
and narrow churchyard.

You had spent the previous day sending
slides to New Zealand for your Skype
lecture – which never took place.
For there the earth shook more violently
than in this churchyard, a second quake
in three days, shaking barns and churches
perched on the precarious coast
but – mercifully – giving rise
to not a single funeral.

Theo, 'loved by God'

Lance Corporal Liam Tasker, 26, of the Royal Army Veterinary Corps, was killed in Afghanistan while on patrol with springer spaniel Theo. The dog collapsed later of a seizure.

The Pearly Gates are fiction – fortunately
or some fundamentalist would put up
a notice saying 'No Dogs'.
But no creature can be denied entry
– it's an unbroken law – if
it arrives in the arms of another.

Their relationship was simple.
'Go find it,' Liam would say and
the dog went off in a sniffing frenzy
until it stopped at a find. Then
'Leave!' Liam would yell
as he came up to identify a bomb.

Together they found fourteen
devices in five months, saving countless
lives. Afterwards Theo was patted and
praised, calmed with smuggled treats,
kept close and comforted until
their next sortie over the hostile sand.

Then came the day with no shout of 'Leave'.
Ears cocked, Theo looked in vain
for Liam until other soldiers came
to drag it back to barracks,
a distraught dog, its barking still
unanswered, its heart broken.

It lives on in military memories,
a war hero more than pet or mascot,
but also remembered by normally dog-
averse Afghans who used to stop their football
to stare at the zigzagging creature
and imitate: 'Leave, Theo, leave!'

This is the Record of John

i.m. Rev. John Hammersley 1936-2006

We sang that Gibbons anthem for Advent,
with you as soloist – your toothy grin I remember
as you hit the high note:
and the Jews sent priests and Levites from Jer-usalem –
from Jer-ooo-salem.
The theological lot loved your choice
of music but expelled you for asking awkward questions.
Like that other John, you became a voice

that crieth in the wilderness.

But the North was no wilderness for you,
neither the famous/infamous flats creeping up the hill
from Sheffield station, nor a revamped new
parish in Lincoln (far from the cathedral).
You became chaplain to shop assistants in Gateshead,
a pokey chapel in the Metro Centre mall,
all the while making word music in your head,
published later as modern psalms for all.

Your psalms were far removed from the polite
Evensong chants in cathedrals; you celebrated diversity –
black skins alongside white, and the darkness of the night
in which the stars are revealed. You found moments
of glory in motorways and mountains, in having to wait at
bus stops – like Quakers waiting on God –
and you didn't find it odd that Moses could not
look on God's face and had to live life backward.

Your psalms of life were all embracing –
you quoted Mandela and Hammarskjold, another
Africa hero, Lavinia Byrne, outspoken ex-nun,
and Anselm who wrote of Jesus as our mother.
One of your psalms celebrated the Millennium
and the breaking down of the Berlin Wall.
You knew of the barriers and setbacks to freedom
"a dying snake will always wriggle."

The snake in your life was the cancer
that delayed your marriage to your MP Ann,
widow and widower, joined in the fight against
prejudice and ignorance. You died less than
a year later. We bade you farewell in true nonconformist
manner - friends, left-wingers, nobody great or
particularly good in St Andrew's Psalter Lane.

Figures in a Landscape

The landscape is a crescent in Bath,
the Crescent, later called the *Royal Crescent*
after a Prince came calling. One of the figures
is a Prince, splendid in cotton robes
which shine in the sun white against the Georgian
stone. It's early morning but his highness
is on Saudi time, has a plane to catch,
ordered a private tour because he'd fallen in love
with Jane Austen when at Eton. Or was it Harrow?
The second figure, the one who serves up
the comparison with Prince Frederick, Duke
of York and Albany, wishes he was still in bed
but he's proud of his Blue Badge and battles
on about Ionic columns, rusticated stone facings,
gamblers, rakes, blue stockings and the Ha-ha.
Did Jane Austen …? Not that we know, Sir,
but they did film *Persuasion* here
for television … some episodes, at least.

The Blue Badge puzzles about the other's
real interest. Perhaps he is planning
a Royal Crescent in Riyadh, surmounted
by a Star and Crescent.
But there's little time for fantasy; the Roman
Baths await, exclusively – expensively –
opened at dawn with a fiat from the
Foreign Office. A large car with a pennant
draws up – silently, of course.

Another figure appears, distant on the
York stone pavement, a woman in a sort
of uniform, Asian. She studies the ground
as she passes. The Prince does not notice her.
Why should he? Domestics are ten a penny
in Riyadh – twenty per riyal perhaps.
But she sets the Blue Badge thinking –
wondering whether he could interest her
in the history of Bath? Its architecture, at least.

She would have gone in a year,
to be replaced by a cousin, a neighbour,
anyway a clone. But suppose she stayed,
could she or a daughter, granddaughter,
learn to love the history of his beloved Bath?
Does heritage mean as much to
a menial as to a millionaire, as much
to an immigrant as a tourist –
unless they'd been to Eton. Or Harrow perhaps.

Young Lions

There's a group of them on the path in front –
five maybe six, it's difficult to tell.
They are larking about – jostling, daring, pushing.
I'm worried: will I get past or have to go between?
They're Asian, so they may have been radicalised –
there's a lot about that in the papers.
Perhaps they'll attack a poor, lone white man.
At least make him walk near the canal's edge.

They stand back to let me pass.
'All right, then, Governor?' 'He's not
your governor; you should call him Sir.'
'I'm not a Sir or a Governor.'
'All right then, Mister?' We all laugh.
I walk on, relieved and more than a bit ashamed.
The sun comes out from behind a cloud,
the Asians resume their jostling.

At their age our group from the Grammar
used to lark about in the park,
snatching each other's satchels and throwing them
in a circle. We made a great deal of noise and got
rebuked. I think we said 'Sorry, Mister or Missus.'
Maybe Sir, but never Governor. The best bit
was the silent laughter afterwards as the old geezer
walked off. 'All right then, Mister?'

Still an Issue

She's young, smiles and stands for seven hours
a day, except when the store allows her to sit – then
she nods off as she did frequently when
pregnant. Both times! She has her regulars,
motherly types who stop for a chat rather than
to buy the Big Issue, though some do. She's
an immigrant, a Roma born in Czecho ...
she hesitates, knowing it's two countries now.

I give her money – partly from guilt because Gran
used to say 'gypos' were dirty, would never answer
the door when they knocked with their posies.
Swore they stole children. Those were
the post-war years, when we were learning
of the Holocaust of Jews. Only later did we
know what Hitler did to the Gypsy Roma.
It was all a long while ago of course.

But not for the Roma. In the capital city
of the same name, Salvini vowed to drive
them out of Italy. In Sicily they burned a truck
of food for Travellers' children.
Hostility in Hungary is a hundred times worse.
Could it happen here? Well, anti-Semitism
is now the trend. In such an environment
can persecuting Roma be far behind?

The Open Hand

It's the daily gauntlet of drivers today –
two lines of parked cars, end to end,
where a door can fling open or a little kid may
dart out from the grip of its mother's hand.

Worse – another car may appear ahead.
Will it wait or advance in a modern joust,
bumper to breastplate, headlamp to headlight,
daring each other to a steel-clashing test?

If you think this fanciful, you may reflect
that the average battle of the War of the Roses
took much the same toll of the maimed and dead
as the annual carnage on an English road.

Fortunately, inside that bright armoured pile
is a driver anxious to get home safe
instead of a knight of bravado and guile.
So politeness wins over saving face.

One waits for the other and is thanked as such
by the raising of an open hand – the best
gesture, better than a headlights flash,
and far more effective than a mailed fist.

A very old Love

It's so convenient. Out of the door,
a clink and the car winks back,
ignition on and one's away. We pass
bus-stop queues and wonder if they're
underprivileged or environmentalists.

We never had a car but Dad worked
in motor parts and had an Industry Day
pass for the first post-war Motor Show.
He chatted and I collected brochures,
glossy books about the smiling, new models.

And smile they did – a familiar, headlamp
eyed, bumper-under-bonnet smile,
in character according to each one's make:
the smart Austin Princess, dashing Standard
Vanguard, homely Oxford Princess.

Cars were the dream world. Reality was
buses where upstairs everyone smoked,
trams which lurched and had yellow
windows to shield the conductor, and

bicycle wheels being caught in the grooves.

Still if you owned a car – so I'm told –
motoring on the trunk roads was sheer
delight. AA men saluted your badge,
petrol cost a pittance and there was never
a problem finding somewhere to park.

Nostalgia for those rare car days is like
all nostalgia. What we yearn for is what we
and few others had, that privileged past.
In the future, no one will yearn for our present,
for traffic jams, diversions, gridlock, pollution.

Lady Wisdom

for Dinah Livingstone

Camden's queen of Common Words,
poet *sans pareil*, tutor to the unmetred,
katabasic publisher of the down-to-earth
if not the underground (Northern Line or otherwise)
       yet – as if all that were not enough
       to admit you to Elysium –
       you strive Calliope-like to engage with God
       or at least with God's fugitives.

On the tossing, fathomless Sea of Faith
you took the tiller and steered for the Bosphorus shore
where *Hagia Sophia*, Holy Wisdom, embodies
all creeds and none – so it is with your Sofia.
       I want to call you Wisdom's handmaid,
       niece or godchild but Google warns me away
       from them, and the Daughters of Wisdom
       are cosily middleclass Catholic.

So Dinah it shall be – daughter of Jacob and Leah
but with brothers bent on blood sports, and
without going into salacious detail
Dinah's name stands for vindication.

Dinah: vindicated in Common Words,
in poetry and the publishing of others,
vindicated most of all in the down-to-earth
dispensing of Wisdom

Heptonstall

Here is the high ground of poetry
where latest Arvon arrivals wander
across the headstone chequerboard till
one sights Sylvia's slab – third from left
second row back – and all wonder
at its unkempt keeping, artificial flowers,
the lighter lead of the Hughes name after
feminist assaults. They pass on up cobbles
to open skies and the crease in the landscape
where they will learn to make poetry --
three words one way, two back.

Another leaves the heaven stall
hurrying slipping on the snow clutching
at arm-wrenching rails on her rush
for the seven o'clock to Rochdale.
In the higgle of dissenters' stones Jabez
born 1821 asks "what woke us?"
"It's the redheaded always late lass"
and his wife leans against his side.
Not yet into poetry the girl continues
down skeltering from Heptonstall
storing memories, stories until
they will tumble out headstrong –
a hundred words one way, none back.

Poems and Parsnips

Poetry apparently makes nothing happen,
according to the wisdom of Wystan Auden.
So if fine words butter no parsnips,
sweeten no swedes, mash no turnips,
then the sharpest poems cut no ice,
not as far as you'd ever notice.

They take no hostages, take no chances,
spare no expense nor claim expenses,
save no souls, seek no redress,
apportion no blame and, even less,
appoint no judges to deal with the grudges
that arise from comments in literary pages;

they have no appetite, feel no fear
and whatever evil they see and hear,
they speak no evil, but first do no harm;
they give no quarter, raise no alarm,
break no bones, yet make no bones
about being written in the obscurest of tones.

They ignore the noes of this negative world –
no through road in rhyme would just be absurd;
no cycling, no walking, no entrance, no exit,
are quite unpoetical – no kidding, no sweat!
Poems will give no thought for the morrow,
whether in hope, excitement or sorrow.

For poets themselves have no regrets –
the Muse dries up, they take no more bets.
Make no mistake, a failing voice
leaves most working poets with no choice
but to write furiously all the more
until their poor families cry out "No more".

A poet should not be massaging facts
in politics, business, cookery or sex.
No, Wystan, old man – a poet's duty
is not start-ups but meaning … and beauty.

Poppies

They're intrusive, an invasion of pop-ups –
shoot-ups from nowhere, ones and twos,
then a crowd of glistening jade,
their heads hanging like shy children.
Soon they dominate the garden,
heads reared, proud, open, puce.

They're not the rose-red poppies of Monet's
cornfields or Flanders – poppies for remembrance.
These are flowers for forgetting:
opium poppies, luxuriant floating silk
enclosing a mass of stamens
the bees swarm to harvest.

Soon gone. As Tam O'Shanter found,
'you seize the flower, its bloom is shed'.
In its place, a seed pod fat as any dome
in Helmand or Kabul, not far from
the opium fields no army
has ever suppressed.

Hydrangea

They crowd the wall, these fresh-faced
offspring of a much travelled mother,
grown from a cutting from my brother's
city garden, wrapped in the damp opinions
of *The Scotsman*, brought south
in the boot to Hertfordshire.

My sibling had done something similar
years before, with a cutting from
the proud hydrangea Dad grew against
his New Town fence, blooming true
blue from the chemicals he'd bought
mail-order in Hertfordshire.

Like many migrants of ancient heritage,

my hydrangea has wayward
thoughts about location and colour –
blue in Labourite Hemel Hempstead,
in Edinburgh faintly pink and against
a wall in rural Hertfordshire bright red.

Wanting Blue

We wanted sky blue – deeply, darkly,
beautifully blue – and were told
it's out of stock and there's no delivery
scheduled. Perhaps we'd prefer gold?

So we took gold from a jazzman's horn
played in Louisiana's summer rain
in the gloomy streets where the blues were born
and saw our blue on wet black skin.

We were offered silver in a lightning strike
splitting a tree too close to home,
engulfing with fire an ancient oak
and saw our blue in the rising flame.

Lead was next, inert and dull,
but lethal and swift in modern gunfire,
in the explosion of bombs which conspire to fill
the air with strokes of steel sapphire.

We looked in glass for the blue of the sky
and found it at last in *la grande cathédrale
de Reims* where the sky's truest blue
shines out from the windows of Marc Chagall.

Self-Portrait

We've all had to do it the same –
hang a mirror on the wall and stare
at ourselves for longer than any sane
person can bear – our only protection
the painter's oath sworn in red wine
that no face is any different
from shadows on a mountainside
or a misshapen melon.

That Hampstead Rembrandt could easily
be a baker waiting for the yeast to rise,
there's Cezanne examining his hat not
his heart and as for Picasso – I thought
at first he portrayed, no betrayed
the shifty man he knew he was
but, no, those were his odd eyes years.
Just look at his Gertrude Stein.

So maybe I'm no true artist feeling
uncomfortable at my reflection
without disguise of shaving foam or hat
but wait! Here I see myself
in a self-portrait of Kokoschka
where the eyes are no painterly device
but windows into a world where
guilt pain loves and loss sit
at the artist's elbow nudging him
nagging him making him nervous.

O Oskar, your world was so much
like ours drifting around rocks of
Freud and fear, archdukes
and angst; we smile at those
antique perils losing our inhibitions
in psychology. Painting is a way of seeing
you said and I affirm that that is so.
Yours is the signed self-portrait
that shows me the way,
Oskar Kokoschka – OK.

A Close Shave

When I was young and winsome
close shaves were decidedly in.
The pick of the prettiest ladies
longed to stroke a chap's smooth chin.

Beards were for sailors and stayabeds,
trapping their breakfast morsels,
or for pirates and Elizabethans
proud of doublets and their dorsels.

The rest of us merriest of mortals
were subjects of the tyrant razor
with improved triple-blade bullies
shaving as close as a laser.

But then came professional stubble,
a day's growth for designer men
so I thought I'd just not take the trouble
to shave and show her … but then

'Not on you, you're too old,' she said
with a peel of lilting laughter,
'you'd look like a poor homeless man
that nobody's looking after.'

And there was Light

At night the oaks and hornbeams
of Post Wood sport an aurora,
leakage from the lights of London.
I always looked the other way
to study the night sky, or at least I did
until the Vicar installed floodlighting
to reduce insurance premiums:
"Let there be light," he proclaimed,
"and there was light" – smugly smiling.

A third of the human race
can no longer see the Milky Way
because of light pollution –
and our culture suffers. What of
Milton's "broad and ample road"
or Hera breastfeeding Heracles and letting
her milk stain the sky?
Not only culture – light pollution
cocoons us to our narrow planet.

In older, unlit times men and women
looked to the sky and acknowledged their place
in the universe: "when I consider the heavens,
the work of thy fingers,
the moon and the stars which thou hast made,
what is man that thou art mindful of him,
and the son of man that thou visitest him?"
As they say, light was the life of men
and not a device to reduce expenditure.

Life in the Gaps

My eyes wander across the walls
passing the window – slab
after slab after slab. Then a gap:
the glimpse of a distant world,
natural, nuanced, bright – but brief.
I stare at the glass, willing there to be
another gap. But the walls crowd out
anything that's not concrete.

It's the surprise of the gap that
grabs you by the throat –
unexpected yet expectant –
like the concrete cloud cover
that seems to be set for the day
when suddenly there's a gap
and enough blue to make trousers
as they say, for short-legged sailors.

I think of the moment
at a concert when the conductor
raises his baton and all is silent –
a gap never to be repeated
for breaks between movements
are not gaps but a convenient pause
for coughing and unmusical noise.

In the night sky Aboriginal people
see shapes in the gaps between stars,
animals pushing aside the brightness
to settle down and sleep –
more natural than the join-the-dots
of our Zodiac. I wonder how many
creature may be curled
in the gaps between these words?

But gaps cannot exist alone –
they need the slabs, the clouds,
the cluttered Zodiac to be gaps.
Like poets, they are the oddities,
the bits of the building the builder
forgot – where patches of bare
earth may grow a jungle – perhaps
even to go deep and overthrow
the slabs that now pass the window.

Render

I must have been ten when I began
to ponder about the word 'render',
when a teacher read – in a voice like thunder:
"Render unto Caesar the things that are Caesar's
and unto God the things that are God's".

But what did it mean to render? I asked
(eyes full of wonder) to which an uncle replied:
"Look boy, yonder, at that sad old house
with the flaking mortar render. It needs
new render and sooner than later."

None the wiser, I went to find the cook
(our family former child minder)
and asked her what it meant to render.
She couldn't have been kinder and said
it was all a matter of melting down the fat.

So bemused I returned to the teacher
who said to render was to give back –
only grander – as Our Lord commanded:
"Render to no man evil for evil,
but render good even to them that hate you."

Which makes me wonder about the war
against terror and extraordinary rendition.
Are the suspects being returned to sender
or is it really a matter of retribution?
Who is rendering what – and what for?

What now?

I sit before the empty page
waiting for a thought worth sullying
the white for. It can take an age
now, but at one time how
the ideas came helter-skeltering out –
like kids at playtime.

I sit in the silent pew
waiting for a prayer worth bending
the knee for. They are very few
now, but at one time how
confessions came cascading down –
like rain in winter.

I sit before an accusing judge
waiting with my brain turning
over past days to pledge
my innocence now, but how
different from the past excuses –

that dropped like windfalls.

I sit wondering why hesitation
has paralyzed each part of my life.
Is age the only explanation?
Or is it that now I have learned how
gabbiness must give way to getting
it right the first time?

Someone To Watch Over Me

The look over the shoulder, the eye
at the keyhole, ear behind the door
are thought of now as prying
into the private, invading as they say
in this boundaries-are-sacred world
– someone's privacy.

Somehow – I don't know how or when –
privacy became a religion,
on a level with human rights,
freedom of belief, our daily bread.
We may treasure new freedoms to roam
except where Keep Out signs are read.

It was always like this – for some.
Armed retainers on the lord's estate
kept the peasants in their place – out!
Privacy for the few. Now in this democratic
world privacy signs seem to sprout
like daffodils in springtime.

If you want to avoid the crowds,
it's best to take a private tour – it will
make you exclusive, enjoying what the masses
cannot enjoy – of which they're de-prived.
Privacy at a price. Worse it's now decreed
public space can become private land.

Yet – in the golden world of memory –

there was no need for privacy.
It was foreign to our nature, our daily lives.
We lived and grew by being un-private
like the young sparrow which learns its song
by eavesdropping as older birds converse.

We were safe – without CCTV or satellite
monitoring – because we were communal,
sharing, listening, overhearing, even eavesdropping
on our betters. Less privacy, less loneliness.
Everyone had someone to watch over
them – or felt they had.

Whether it was God, our mother, a teacher,
elder sibling or friend, security was
assured in a Utopia of Openness.
We could certainly regain it except –
it would mean breaking down guarding walls,
even before we tried to convert those cowering within.

The Tree within a Tree

At a certain point on the river bank there is
a tree – you'd need daylight to spot
it and even then you might not.
It has all the appearance of strong growth
but in fact it's dead and the growth
is a new tree trapped within the trunk
of the old and that too may die if the trunk
collapses instead of crumbling away.

The man knows this but does not tell the woman:
she is not from these parts and would say
he spoke in metaphor. They walk in silence,
late swans floating by with the end of the day.
They pass couples relaxed with wine in boats
anchored stern to stern for security. The walkers
are relaxed but not secure. Friends call them a couple –
firmly rooted, copious years together. They call
themselves friends, not even lovers though they have
just made love.

What they had had, what friends
saw, think they can still see, is all
quite dead. There is growth within the shell
of decay, shooting unexpectedly for them though
friends take it for granted. The man and woman know
this, it is their secret. She will let things take
their course, he puzzles by what means he can make
sure the young tree survives.

Blossom Time

In Barnard Park you remarked on the blossom
how it could well be confused with snow;
now you are high above the ocean
en route to a land where for all I know
there may be blossom, there may be snow –
America's seasons confuse me so.

You left with a show of great affection
but confessed to feelings confused and so
what you felt once may now be fiction,
and I await your return to know
if love lives on to blossom and grow
or now lies dead beneath the snow.

The Silk Cotton Tree*

The last day they sat under a silk cotton tree.
She'd said they had to talk. The waiter said
it was a sacred tree: Mayans believed their dead
climbed through the branches to reach to heaven.

But the trunk was split, held together with wire.
Just as well, he said, or they'd reach different heavens.
After the smiles she said she needed space and strangely
this drew them closer together: their tears mixed
with the condensation on their margaritas.

Later they flew out, passing cocooned from sun
into sudden night, wrapped in sleep and thought
through five thousand miles of space.
The baggage took ages to arrive. They travelled
to London in silence – and there they split.

* or kapok tree (*ceiba pentandra*)

Roses

The roses you gave me were a delicate
delicious pink. At the door, you thrust
them at me, knowing I must
take and admire them before our first
embrace. So I placed them centre table
where they would look their best.

Now they've become the colour of rust
with gold edging each tight petal fist,
textured like the yellowing letters
I first sent you when I admired your lips
and dared not venture a delicate kiss.
Now when I look closer at the roses
I see what at first I had totally missed
that the natural pink is not entirely lost.

How it was

It wasn't supposed to be like this:
the pretty Perpendicular church located
just too close to the mainline so the priest
had to pause for the 1215 to Derby,
the girl band substituting for the organ
to remind us the groom had been lead
guitar in the Ghouls – or was it the Ghosties? –
before he went into computers,
the long delay before the bride's entrance
everyone shuffling in the heat

then the daughter – the one not in the band –
appearing and the chain of whispers:
how it had almost been called off,
how he would certainly have to pay,
how he had shared a room in the village pub
last night with the best man's ex.
It wasn't supposed to be like this,
it would have been quite hilarious
but for the tear on the bride's cheek slowly
dropping to the dress she had made herself.

A Drastic Decline

It would merit big bold type if it were ever
reported – 'Drastic Decline of the Smile
in the West'. For according to
the Institut Guillaume Dechenne,
smiling teachers and midwives are now
33 per cent fewer than ten years ago,
while policemen (41), taxi-drivers on 50,
are humourlessly, joylessly surpassed
only by politicians who are three times more grim.

The data gathered by Dechenne, famous for
smileology studies, measured 'smizing' –
smiling with the eyes, the true smile
that crowfoots the faces of the happy old.
In contrast flexing the muscles
at the corner of the mouth
with no effect on the eye produces
the token smile beloved of our leaders
and air hostesses: the Virgin Atlantic smile.
Worse – for flexing the zygomaticus muscle
also produces a grimace.

Causes range from austerity and Brexit
through an ABC of congenital seriousness to
zygomaticitis – the familiar facial twitch
of the aforesaid muscle.
For once global warming is not thought
to be to blame, but only in the West.
In Asia/Africa the victims of storm
and drought have little to smile
about – now or then.

B Movie

It wasn't a costume thing. They'd tried that once –
her nylons got twisted and his padded shoulders
got him wedged in the Paddington gents.
It was more of a hiccup in their happy hour
when routinely they would tick off the terrors
of their day over a pint and a Pinot Grigio
and then retire to bed with a video
and a take-away.

It was the menacing way he was looking
at them, he with the sallow-face, sagging jaw,
the way he followed them from the bar
stopping when they stopped, clearly a hitman
a Vegas mobster, a deranged stalker
who would bundle her into the back of a black
Buick, cruise up beside him door swinging open:
"Get in. The dame gets it if you squeal".

They gave up the bar, drank in distant dives
looked back at each corner, separated
a block away from where they lived – but
not before he'd pull her into a porch:
"That's something to remember me by".
He would get home first and wait
for her key to turn in the lock then look
at her carefully, how she was flushed
how she caught her breath, had creases
in her skit. He knew she had a lover.

Because

At first it was all beckoning
(he to her) and bonking (he to her ... mainly).
Because ... well, just because!
But the beckoning stopped and somehow
the bonking became becalmed.

Yet they were today people,
they knew the statistics and the strains
their out-of-the-office limitations.
there was no bickering, barracking
no one went barking mad.

They worked at their laptops
sublimating simultaneously
on opposite sides of the lounge –
back-to-back. Not that anyone
would use that term to them.

They were northerners, descended
from denizens of back-to-back
streets ... in Bacup, Blackpool.
They were today people, they still
slept together ... back-to-back.

Ghosts

They're milking the vaults again
blundering through the murk with every
sensor known to media man
and pulling rumour's slippery teats
for spurts of ectoplasm that might
nourish the dying tourist industry.
When foot-and-mouth banned Americans
from the wind-blown fells, then
down to the vaults they had to go.

Ghosts are every season's must-have,
must-see: all small towns need at least
one in their heritage pack and, of course,
every hamlet has its ghost. They're
as common as … well, mists
in March. When they approached me
to lead a ghost walk, I suggested a start
at No 19 where before its makeover
a demobbed Tommy shot his wife and her lover
and no one lived there for 40 years.
They said I wasn't taking the subject seriously.

It's not that I don't believe in ghosts.
I just don't think they're as common as
mobile phones, nor as user-friendly. I have
it on the best authority that no ghost ever
danced obedience to a tour leader, film crew,
wrinkled priest who was everybody's uncle,
long-haired starlet brandishing a crucifix,
tabloid journalist, paranormalist or even poet.

Ghosts come and go as they will – though
not without warning. When I hear the five
oboe notes in *Das Lied Von Der Erde* or
the sax of Charlie Parker I know I'm
in their country where lost liebe Kinder
dance with hollow-eyed heroin users,
yearning for the love that undoes tragedy.
I watch them but they are not my ghosts.

Mine come seldom but then insistently –
the ones whose hopes … whose love I'd
drawn out, cut off, deserted, left to wither,
reproachful spirits that never leave me,
will never be exorcised even when I know the hurt
is forgiven, forgotten, forgone for happiness.

Ghosts are not just for Christmas:
we cannot live without them.

Knife Crime

Knife crime is an issue, a headline:
'Labour attacks Tories over knife crime'.
It's an equation: 'More police = less knife crime.'
It's also a commodity: 'Leicester has less
knife crime than Derby.'

   'How much knife crime would you like today, Madame?'
   'Oh, I don't think I'll have knife crime this week,
                                      thank you.'

Knife crime is a problem but the answer's easy:
stop and search, lock 'em up, make 'em pay.
Lock their stop, pay the lock, whatever …

   'Hey, you, Kid! Do you carry a knife?'
   'A what?'
   'A knife – like a sharp, stabbing weapon.'
   'Oh, you mean a blade. And we don't stab, we shank.
   Look, here, it's in its scabbard so as not to scratch my
   thigh. I wouldn't go out without it. It's for defence
   against a shanking.'
   'But it's dangerous, it could be illegal.'
   'Look, I'd rather go down by twelve than be carried high
   by six – pallbearers, ok?

I suppose it's a status thing like a gentleman's sword, or
a banker's umbrella which they never use, or
a police constable's Tazer.

> *'But can't you see the harm you're doing, Kid?*
> *Can't you see it's illegal?'*
> *'What? You mean like terminating my bro from school,*
> *or stopping me mum's benefits?'*

Knife crime is a public health issue, they say.
 Bhh problem, and Bob's your uncle! It's an epidemic
brought in by immigrants, Asians, other religions, the
unwashed.

> *'Look, it's a dreadful business, of course, but*
> *not anything to do with us or our way of life.*
> *We don't let our children go out at night and*
> *certainly not to the knife crime places – Glasgow, East*
> *London, Brixton, Islington. They are*
> *far away places, of which we know nothing.'*

POEMS OF TRAVEL

The Samos Sea

Do you remember the sunlit Samos sea
and that cove with rock hillocks concealing
the town on one side, an oil refinery
on the other. It may have been man-made
but surely you must remember the first feel
of fish circling about your thighs, followed
by that pair of tutting ducks making sure
their old mum on the beach was not ailing
in the ten minutes they'd been away from her?

To the swimmer it seemed a toy sea with ferries
like bathtime models passing from rock
to rock, but from our rooftop balcony a series
of smokey hills picked out Asia on the far side
of an ocean. We went there – on the way back
Poseidon or his Turkish counterpart played
water polo with our boat. Do you remember
people eating green figs, and green faces on deck
slowly returning to a pale shade of amber?

When we could we swam twice a day,
you walking down in straw hat and sarong.
The stony beach was a small price to pay
for the warm clear water of that tideless cove.
You always liked an extra swim – alone
to contemplate, you said, while I would have
my shower. Do you remember coming back for tea
and we made love, both wet, my courteous tongue
greedy for a last taste of the Samos sea?

Turkish Census Day

For Richard McKane

It was the sabbathest of sabbaths,
twelve hours when the beehive by the Bosphorus
was lethargised, the ancient anthill
of the orient frozen by order
of an authority quite uncomputerised
so that every kindred body
could be counted – children, dogs,
cats, vermin and tourists excepted,
along with the pigeons on the steps
of Sayfeddin Alkan mosque and all the fishes
of the sea of Marmara floating free.

It was a stolen day,
an interruption to lawful mayhem,
a day for shooting stock film of
deserted streets, for sitting in doorways,
for washing curtains, fixing satellite dishes;
a day for the children to play
football in the streets, for watching
foreign films, and doing other things
in quiet rooms. What name will
they give the offspring conceived
on Turkey's census day?

Bothered men with grey forms
searched for ancient addresses,
knocking on gates of empty lots.
A woman in leather sat among
a large, laughing family, making
each adult painstakingly sign.
r
A child perched on a hip watched on.
Will her children's children
see that census form, grafting
it into their proud family tree?
Will they too have censuses?
Will they play in empty streets?

A GENOESE TRIPTYCH

La Superba

It was Petrarch who call Genoa proud
as it vyed with rival Venice, known as *la Serena*,
in war after war. Here Christopher Columbus
tasted boyhood long before he discovered
America. But what does Genoa have to be proud
of today – the Duomo, the Palazzos Doria
and Rosso, the Porto Antico?
For me it's *focaccia*, finessed with local cheeses,
or Genovese pesto made with pecorino cheese,
pine-nut kernals and basil, served with *troffie* or
the other pastas of the Ligurian coast. And
of course, there is the white wine of Cinque Terra
and the red of Dolceacqua.   Superb!

Circonvalmonte

The indicator on the yellow bus
offers a round tour of valley and hills.
We would prefer the funicular but
there are no trains in winter, just rusting rails –
so we select a *salita*, start to climb
past apartments and patios pausing to look
at the unrolling map of the port's outline
where a child's model ferry begins to dock.
We stop surprised as finches flock
and admire the bright orange bricks
picked out in moss beneath our feet –
bricks laid carefully for walking;
here the houses are made of concrete.

At the top the grey walls of the Genoese
Republic defend the city now against armies of
factories, motorways, a domino set of other hills
backed by the Alps – the halberds and Renaissance
banners are in some museum below:
in their place mobile-phone masts sprout
from fenced-off plots. A salient for artillery

and stacks of cannon balls is ankle-deep
in coke cans and condoms. The sole defence
left on this strategic ridge is latex.

It's a busy ridge – small cars, Pandas and
Peugeot vans take to these hills, all driven
by lone males. And Piaggia scooters
whose riders stop, remove their helmets and stare.
Are they admiring the view, looking for the
neighbour's wife, recalling summer conquests,
and counting past condoms? Fresh conquests
are forbidden – *'Divieto di Caccia'*. Best to do
a little circuit of the hills – *Circonvalmonte* –
and then freewheel down to lunch.

Pietra magica – Nervi, New Year's Day

A child has wiped the magic slate clean
erased the hot hues of summer, the ochre
grass on the hills driving down to the town
where in umber shadows cool-seeking couples
licked *cone gelati – nocciola croccantino
ciocolato –* lounging along the *passagiata,*
its bricks baked a brighter shade of brown
and below beside a green-brown sea
bronzed bodies spread along the rocks
skin shining with oil, skin so brown
the breasts were nippleless.

The wiped slate should now be blank and bland
but its white is wild, whipped up and turbulent –
mare spumante, foaming spume, the sperm
of a frenzied Neptune beating against the rocks
to penetrate and produce new seas.

Rivers in Portugal

1. The Douro

Tourists on the Cais da Ribeira might think
it's put on for them – the cresting waves
making antique barques rock at anchor,
a river-ocean meeting – not always mild.
In the port lodges they point to flood marks
metres over our heads – higher, dizzily high
the archbishop's palace clings
to a rock face the Douro spared.

For tourists and guests of his Grace
the lodges are labelled in three metre letters
of companies pumping out Porto's lifeblood
to Wall Street clubs, gouty Oxford dons:
Sandeman Taylor Cockburn and Croft,
familiar names on our Christmas screens
that boost the flow of the ruby river.

No deity decreed that the Douro divide
port wine from people – commerce from creed –
or that a church should perch like a granite
boulder on every avenued hill while beneath
in crevices live the poor – frying fish
in the streets. Only the feast of São João
lightens their lives – jokey São João
when everyone hits his neighbour with squeaky
plastic hammers.

2. The Lima

We crossed the Lima on the one o'clock ferry
to Elysian dunes of waving grass
salt-and-pepper sand made silver
by glinting crustacean specks
minute flowers making rainbows in miniature
and the Atlantic's base beat
making forgetting easy.
Later we learned that Roman legions

believed the Lima was the Lethe,
that they'd forget families and friends if
they crossed, a story stitched
in the tawny tapestry on the hotel wall
with the consul wading across
shouting out individual names
to show he had not forgotten.

We lazed on the shore like Romans
cossetted by the crystal dunes,
emptying our minds of enemies
ephemera everything that might have crept
unpacked into our luggage, feasting
on forgetting, until the wind turned.
The young boatman, unlike Charon,
had given us return tickets.

3. The Minho

Wide water green as olives
lapping the tussocks of two nations;
boys fish from the shadows
a single sculler skims the surface of
the chessboard river stretched out
from mountains to sea.

History by the Minho is now a game:
queens are remembered for conquering
kingdoms off the board; a bishop
blocked by his own king, terrible
Torquemada sits puffily in a chapel
eyeing territory he could never torture;
converted castles are floodlit for pawns
to come across and spend.

At either end of the girdered bridge
customs-posts crumble as if a warring
horde had passed this way.
Pay in pesetas or escudos they say
but euros built the motorway that crosses
the winking water in two blinks of the eye.

The Mendelssohn-Haus

How could Victoria's favourite composer
avoid Victorian clutter and live in such an elegant
Biedermeier flat? But this was Felix
by name, felix by nature, the happy one
the charmer, adorer of Shakespeare,
painting his travels in watercolours and music,
worshipping both wife and sister –
              who could not love him?
Well, Wagner for one – the jealous womaniser
who waited till Felix was dead
to attack Judaism in music – all tinkling tunes,
no depth, no resonance of the Folk Spirit.

Thank you, cocky Dick. We know what
happened to your Folk Spirit in Nuremburg
and it wasn't just the Mastersingers who mastered
the spirit of the master race. You did not harm
Mendelssohn but you murdered something
for which his music stood – Europe's culture
open to all peoples, religions, races,
the passion of a baptised Jew who rediscovered
Bach's passion according to St. Matthew
proud to be Mendelssohn, a rabbi's grandson.

There are still little Wagners around
hissing anti-semitism under their breath
and then there is Sharon, telling Jews
to flee Europe for shelter in his belligerent
theocracy. Oh Felix, we need you now,
your bright tunes, your optimism
that spirit which gleams from the desk
where you composed.

In Search of JSB

The biggest Bahnhof in Europe
where the rail rivals of Saxony, Prussia
built two stations, now a three-tiered

mall (capitalism comes back to Leipzig)
but no hint here of Father Bach,
no poster, no cantata to make you quicken your step:
Kommt, eilet und laufet, ihr flüchtigen Füsse
You must go deep into the tram-ringed city.

In the Rathaus there's a room
where he signed on for 27 years' music;
there's his contract and a scowling man
who's eaten too much -- that can't be him.
Zimmerman's Coffeehouse and concerts
are no more, instead there's a cosy
coffee boutique where tourists sit and
sip and listen to the Coffee Cantata --
too baroque for him.

To the vaulted Thomaskirche
where his fingers fugued over the keys,
waved in the Thomaschor in cantata
after cantata. There's another fat man
in bronze outside, inside a distant figure
imprisoned in prisms of glass --
too far away to know if that's him.
But people queue to do the tour
everyone seeking his own Bach --

he of the Masses or the Brandenburgs,
partitas and Passions, the Air on a G String
played as jazz, the Goldbergs
interpreted by Gould.
Mine was a young man's Bach, the Passion
According to Matthew sung by students
from the gallery of a small church in Westphalia --
the height of the Cold War and two
National Servicemen walking back to barracks
talking Bach, Bach, Bach.

Leipzig demolished the Thomasschule,
so you can't touch the table
where sons, daughters, pupils copied
the Matthew Passion in manuscript,

Anna Magdalena writing with the rest --
pregnant as usual. The school's gone
but young people still stop to gossip --
violin and oboe cases easy under their arms,
a cello balanced on a bicycle.

Bach in the Kreuzkirche, Dresden

Grey hair, grey beards, anoraks and scarves –
what pictures flood their minds and colour
the music, what memories are stirred by the organ
in this church of broken stone?
The sort of private religion the communists
allowed sheathed the shattered pillars
in concrete – subdued services, rough-cast pietism.
And so it's remained: the capitalist gilding
of Dresden stops at the huge doors.

What memories are stirred by the organ
in this darkened church? If they
were here and survived, do the fire-storm generation
still blame the British: the cross of nails
from Coventry was a gesture of shame
as much as sharing. How do they balance
the past: Nazis, RAF bombers, Stasi?
Does a Bach fugue put life thoughts to flight,
cleansing them with counterpoint?

Or are the listeners in this temple
no different from audiences anywhere,
as they halve heaven with the here-and-now,
pondering "what shall I give Hans
for supper" mixed with the indelible,
undeniable memory of first hearing Bach
on a keyboard so much smaller than
 the mighty organ in the Kreuzkirche?

Nazareth

One can be easily overwhelmed by the Basilica
of the Annunciation – a huge art gallery
of every nation's representation of the angel
addressing an astonished Mary.
But I remember Nazareth more from for trudging
up and down a dusty road looking
for a jacket and a lost Oyster card.

I had spent enough time in the Basilica
to merit a meal (I admit) with wine – an Arab café
by the bustling bus station. Then to kill time
a saunter around the trinket shops for
mementoes bearing Nazareth's name,
my bag hanging from my shoulder, the coat
slung over it, containing well – just the Oyster card.

I discovered my loss and rushed from shop to shop
asking 'Has anyone found an old brown coat' –
I was joined by a boy who said he would interpret.
He fared no better in Arabic than I in English. I tried
explaining about the Oyster card but he smiled and said
shellfish were not found in that part of the Middle East.
Before I caught the bus, I gave him a coin.

Jacob's Creek

Been there, done that, seen it,
the brown stream flecked with foam
next to the winery which now flows
over all our supermarket shelves,
you and your camera dodging cars,
four-wheel drives, roo-bars rearing.

We called at a cellar door, so-called
to seduce the passing trade,
tasting from six strange bottles
mini-glasses for those on mini-tours,

and queasily bought a box of two
for the quaintness of the detailed labels.

But no brochure prepared us for
the valley veiled in winter rain,
eucalyptus weeping over the lookout
muddied sheep among the rocks,
or the greater warmth our laughter brought
than all the fine wines of the Barossa.

Glebe Park, Canberra

A park with tall bare oaks, surely foreigners
like me. And this is September.
They have close, straight trunks such as
our common ancestors grew for ship-
building or timber-framed halls – not the
spreading parkland oaks of Humphrey Repton.
These Canberra oaks were all planted together.
Perhaps they came from a New South Wales nursery
founded by a Victorian arborist, or were a cargo of English
saplings shipped in a dry hold so that none sprouted in
the Indian Ocean. In Glebe Park, Canberra, they are part
of the furniture – along with the daffodils,
periwinkle, metal seats and barbecue tables.
They are tolerated by the joggers and liked
by boys seeking last season's acorns.

STROKE POEMS 2018

Autonomy

It's a word that gets the mouth moving –
lips and tongue, tongue, lips,
a word I've just learned or relearned,
I suppose you'd say.
I liked it so much I looked it up,
found it was anchored to what I felt –
not like those free-floating words
the therapist woman throws at me:
lettuce, motorcycle, thermometer.
I read them all right but can't see them.

I liked autonomy so I looked it up –
and was puzzled. 'Self-rule' *yes*, 'Self-determination' –
yes, that's what I lived for, but 'Independence'?
No, that's where I differed from former friends:
the ones who went into exile to avoid arrest,
the others who talked of 'taking back control'.
They saw me as an old fogy, a compromiser,
                                    a back-peddler.
They lost of course but so did we all. The autonomy
we'd achieved over decades of hard work
was caught up in their defeat, floating off
with the bubbles of so-called freedom. It was
some time ago, of course, and normality
(as our new masters call it) has been restored.

I remember all that because it's me, a paradigm
of me – rescued from collapse, given a new life.
They rushed to my rescue – children, brothers, sisters,
therapists galore, even a concerned postman.
Changes were made: a regular cleaner,
hand-free gadgets, life-saving alarms.
The fridge was scoured of everything
past its sell-by date – quite right except that
I habitually shopped at the reduced displays.
How lucky I am, surrounded with love and attention.

Smiled upon by circumstance and fortune <u>but</u> –
there is a but. It's not independence I miss:
no man is an island in this interconnected world.
It's autonomy, that word redolent of at least
feeling self-sufficient – something,
I'm told, I can no longer expect – after a stroke.

Forgotten

I'm puzzled by my loss of memory,
the sudden cull of my vocabulary.
Some words arrive unbidden –
like school friends you'd hoped you'd forgotten.
Others struggle to attach themselves
to what I can see or hear or think.
Things I know I've long valued and
long to name remain nameless, orphans.
Flowers mostly, more than people.
You can get away with not naming people:
their vanity will let the cat out of the bag
sooner or later –
but flowers are not vain: even the brightest
lack all boastfulness. I tour my garden,
struggling to put names to plants I've planted,
nursed through frost and draught, loved.
I stand before a bloom, willing it
to reveal its name, the common name that
friends know it by, let alone the Latin –
but there is no answer. Some do speak
or I imagine they do. The boastful rose is one,
nature's exception. And the grass. For the rest,
the centuries that went into the naming of plants,
my proud achievement as a child
and adolescent gardener, are all now lost.

Repartee

I was known for shooting from the lip,
the fastest tongue in the West, so to speak!

But apologies for a start which seemed slick
though it took a whole afternoon to compose –
a case of spontaneity which ain't –
and that's the point of this poem – or shall I say 'elegy'?

A quick tongue and a quicker pair of heels
were my school certificate. So with Joe, that giant German
from Finland who I teased as a pseudo-Nazi
not knowing until years later that his family
were victims of Stalin first. Or that job
where I was sacked for my banter –
the sit-on-his-hands boss said we'll decide tomorrow or
maybe next week – or next year,
I quipped. He said I was bloody rude
and so I bloody was …. but it just slipped out.

But no longer. A blockage now impedes
the flow – wit waylaid, my repartee restrained.
It's not as if I don't have a response, or don't see
the funny side of it all: it's just late arriving,
it's there to be savoured later at leisure –
esprit d'escalier – I realise now
it's much better that way.

Not just for me but for a wider world perhaps.
How second thoughts might deepen debate,
make politics more palatable,
the listening mode instead of 'point of order',
might make the markets pause and be
more mature, might restrain the guns
while communication prospered –
no more shooting from the hip, so to speak.

It's a tall order, I know. Not everyone
is blessed with my advantages –
to have had time to regret those school yard quips,
to have come back from the disgrace of the sack,
to have learned to love and live with my stroke.

POEMS IN LOCKDOWN

Ash Wednesday 2020

How appropriate now that
they've cancelled Carnival in Barcelona and Cadiz,
proscribed the public kiss in Paris,
vetoed the masked melee of Venice –
though most people are wearing masks of course –
because we cannot hope to party again,
because we cannot hope . . .

Remember you are dust and to dust
you shall return. But, Father, I want real ash,
not dust or an incinerated last year's cross,
and not just on my forehead,
but ash on my face and body.
Lord, not only my feet, said Peter ...
and got a dusty answer.

But real ash is reserved for fire-fighters
in Victoria, New South Wales, snatching
and clutching scarred koalas from the flames –
scared and scarred little bears.
Ash reserved for those who fared through
fire, fearless among the flames, not sitting
under a juniper tree in the cool of the day.

It's no longer an annual midweek rite,
but the everyday fête – and fate –
of mankind, animal kind, every kind
of God's creatures – if there is a God
who cares for small bears.
A rite no longer celebrated by
expatriate laureates, old men.

The young march in thousands to hear
an improbable small teen from Sweden
who eschews air travel, speaks truth to power,
her voice heard in schools of every nation.

The coronavirus is not her friend,
but like her it has shaken the foundations:
Ash Wednesday can never be the same again.

Distancing

I never thought I'd be distancing
from you, my closest of all close
mates of mind and mood, the one I've
breathed, whispered and kisspered
with for so many years.

But we distance to survive
become close when no breath can
pass between us, you perched on
a camp chair, the window between,
while I articulate and admire inside –
a good thing the glass is clean.
I see your lips a bare two metres
away, moving as you laugh and speak,
but never to frame a kiss.

It's better – this distanced love –
than electronic speech or the video which
freezes your lips while you go on speaking.
Better than the war which some compare
this lockdown to. In the war, with little else to do
on board, my Dad wrote long letters to his soulmate,
Mum. He could not say – or did not know –
where they were going but they did contain
poems of certain, surest love,
bringing them closer together
as the distances grew greater.

Disobediently different

The lockdown is meant to stop us
individuals moving closer to other individuals
within two metres – the distance they say

the virus can leap or fly. Families, couples
are excused as no longer individuals.

But what about getting closer in spirit,
infecting each other with laughter or
subversively individual thoughts, ways
of breaking out of the lockdown into
a disobediently different world?

What about time-travelling to
a saner, sunnier world, a real distance
from this predictable present. They put on
old films to keep us locked in but what
if we could reshoot them in real time?

That Hitchcock film shows Doris Day
foiling a murder in the Albert Hall –
a coating of culture for a thin thriller.
But what if you and I could be there
caressing to the Well-Tempered Clavier?

So much owed by so many

They're comparing the virus pandemic
to the last war – one ex-sufferer says
the Spitfire pilots of today are the NHS heroes.
Quite right too. *Never was so much owed
by so many to so few.* And you can parse Winny's
words any way you like – so few doctors,
so few nurses, too few coronavirus tests.
We weren't prepared for the pandemic
nor in 1939 were we really prepared for war.

But it's the 1945 comparison that will
be crucial – when we British turned
our backs on Winny and voted for a different
Britain – for the welfare state, nationalisation
of ramshackle railways and private coal,
most tellingly, for Nye Bevan's NHS.
It was a master stroke for so many,

like my Mum and Dad who relied on
savings clubs pre-war, though the benefit
for the many was resisted by Harley Street.

Will something similar happen this time?
There's no shortage of desirables –
fewer polluting air miles, no diesels
near schools, no cruise ship megaliths,
no tax breaks, no fake news, no spin.
Can 'community' be a priority for policy-makers
again, can the values unearthed by the lockdown
be perpetuated nationwide at least?
Can we be prepared for the next crisis,
for living on the edge rather than down the middle?
All things are possible but – beware! –
some remember not 1945, but the depressions
of 1929, 2008 and the corresponding bounce-back.

It had never gone away

We used to think of Nature as the amorphous
background to everything else, a subject for young
children to study, the excusable something everyone
has – their *Nay-cher*. It hardly touched the here and now:
paying the rent, catching a train, voting – well Labour –
anything else is not in my nature.

Then came Covid 19 – real nature making itself
heard and felt, getting its own back perhaps.
Amid the pain and gloom, scientists reported
unheard of changes – fewer pollution clouds seen
from outer space, seismic wobbles no longer wobbling,
the cleanest air since the time of the Beatles.

It seemed incredible and of course temporary.
What would happen when the world was back
at work? OK, a vision of life without fossil fuels,
but when? Then I noticed the butterfly profusion,
bumble bees and blackbirds. Nature returning, but
it had never gone away. It was us that had changed.

Familiarly unfamiliar

It's unfamiliar and yet not strange
because we remember it, we of a certain
age, at least we think we do.
The air is clean because of the lack of traffic
and so is the sound, not a lack of sound,
not silence, but an unfamiliarly familiar
quiet in which things can be heard.

Things like a hosepipe two gardens away,
a small dog barking and then not barking
because no one answered, no planes overhead,
no train, no cars, only the unfamiliarly natural –
blackbirds competing with their different codas,
pigeons being insistent, the small bird
whose song has something to do with bread
and cheese, which you go on the internet
to identify.

A quiet to savour while it lasts, an atmosphere
or environment paid for by the pain
and panic of the viral lockdown, a quiet
that may never be repeated but
will surely be remembered.

Back in time

Suddenly while we were struggling to understand
what the coronavirus is doing
to our present, having brushed aside
fatuous politicians trying to whistle up
the spirits of the Blitz, Dunkirk,
even Crecy, Agincourt and Waterloo,

they said that the economy would take
its worst hit in living memory, then
in a hundred years, two hundred or
even more – worse than after Crecy,
Agincourt or Waterloo. All victories

are won on credit, after all.

So how far back, how fluctuating bad
will it get? They say the oil price has
collapsed and some think that helps
combat climate change, but will we be back
to horses and carts, most people cycling,
some sitting waiting for a horse-drawn Omnibus?

Will we be what we were before they invented
the Empire, an offshore island of smallholders,
keeping chickens, weaving our own woollens,
Darby and Joans, Colin Clout come home again?
All well and good provided we can hold on to
our plumbing, toilet paper and the Ipad.

Be Prepared

Everyone saw it coming – Germans,
scientists, even some who worked at Oxford
but not the Bullingdon gang-ho guys.
They knew better – being prepared might
flatter foreigners and little brown Boy Scouts.
Not for us, the elected, the elite.

We are your leaders, it's we that won
your votes, so forget about that testing,
the masks, goggles and ghastly gowns.
Best just to isolate yourself in an expences-
paid-for pad, with a hamper from Harrods
and the booze to make you senseless.

We're not worried about the exit
from the EU or the lockdown.
We knew better than the horrid *hoi polloi*.
With our shares lodged well off-shore
and our parents out of town,
we are better prepared than the poor.

Remembrance Day 2020

They should have done it years ago,
this self-distancing Cenotaph – Prince,
premier, politicians all spaced out
with their wreaths, no crowds, no marching,
like Flanders and the distancing of no-man's-
land and the wire into the distance stretching.
A recreation of the past as if the virus
remembered our history as well as its own.

Across the Atlantic, crowds sang, danced
and partied at the toppling of a braggard,
not distancing perhaps, but masked at least
as the braggard's bullyboys never were.
Their victory promises a recreation of a lost
but vividly remembered Great Society
of inclusiveness, racial harmony, an
America to lead an admiring world.

You and I abandoned the news, walked to a hillside
where a warm sun failed to dispel the dew
and sat on our coats, glorying in the colours
of autumn. But we were not alone, a mass
of ladybirds descended on coats, arms, heads
in crowds of blues and reds, flexing bright wings
in autumnal defiance. This has been
a November warmer than many can remember.

But the ladybird horde, though glad, carried
a warning, the threat louder by the day
of global warming, of autumn emasculated
by relentless summer, of grass never moistened
with the dew. The victor across the Atlantic
acknowledges this as the braggard never would.
Some believe his election can help rescue the planet,
a distant prospect but at least now there is hope.